I0755455

MILES
O'REILLY
CARLETON-PUBLISHER
N.Y
MDCCCLXIV
PENFIELD-BROSS.

THE

LIFE AND ADVENTURES,

Songs, Services, and Speeches

OF

PRIVATE MILES O'REILLY.

(47th Regiment, New York Volunteers.)

"The Post of Honor is the Private's Station."

With Comic Illustrations by Mullen.

FROM THE AUTHENTIC RECORDS OF THE NEW YORK HERALD.

NEW YORK:
CARLETON, PUBLISHER, 413 BROADWAY.
MDCCCLXIV.

R. CRAIGHEAD,
Printer, Stereotyper, and Electrotyper,
Carton Building,
81, 83, and 85 *Centre Street.*

To

OUR NAVY AND OUR ARMY;

TO

ALL GOOD CITIZENS OF MANHATTAN ISLAND

AND

THE GREAT STATE OF NEW YORK;

AND TO

PATRIOTS OF EVERY CLASS AND NATIONALITY THROUGHOUT THE UNITED STATES,

This Volume is Respectfully Inscribed.

CONTENTS.

LIST OF ILLUSTRATIONS.

PREFACE.

THE Editor of this collection of the writings in which Private Miles O'Reilly, 47th Regiment New York Volunteers, has figured more or less extensively, had hoped, in preparing this volume for the press, to have had the gay and luminous assistance of the young soldier, humble in position, but distinguished by his talents, who forms the central figure and inspiration of every scene, and whose droll merits have been so generously recognized by all classes and parties of the American public. This hope has been suddenly disappointed by the return of Private Miles to his regiment in the Department of the South, where, it is conjectured, he may be employed by Government as the bearer of flags of truce to the Rebel lines. Indeed, there are rumors that his present mission is of a very high diplomatic nature, far surpassing in importance the charge recently conferred on Dr. Zacharie, the famous chiropodist and international negotiator, who has twice visited Richmond as the mutual friend and foot-physician of the United States and Rebel Cabinets. The rumors in this connexion further add that O'Reilly's mission will be reciprocated by the sending of Ex-Generals Gustavus W. Smith and Mansfield Lovell, on behalf of the Richmond Government, to meet our "Irish Ambassador" at Savannah, or Port Royal Ferry, whichever place may be agreed upon. The intrinsic probabilities of this affair are increased by the fact that Private O'Reilly was for several years employed in the Street Department, of New York City, under the Ex-Generals in question, as Inspector, at three dollars *per diem*, of some contract work which never had any existence,—thus making him their friend for life. The Editor, therefore, hopes the very best issue from the negotiations now about to be inaugurated under such happy auspices; and, in the absence of Private Miles, can only refer such readers as may desire to have a personal picture and history of that soldier to the chapter in which is narrated the interview between President Lincoln, his Cabinet, the Foreign Diplomatic Corps and Private M. O'Reilly, towards the conclusion of this volume.

For the rest, a work of this kind needs little preface. Truth, by arraying itself in the garb of humor, may often attract the attention which has been denied to her most serious appeals. The very wide celebrity achieved by the writings of Private Miles O'Reilly is in itself an evidence of the anxious and revolutionary condition of the public mind. Old landmarks are swept away, and men are casting about for new issues and a purer system of public life.

In the discussion of the iron-clad question, forming the earlier portion of this volume, the arguments advanced and the conclusions arrived at, are those of sincerity and deep conviction. Justice is sought to be done to Admiral Du Pont and his gallant subordinates, but certainly not at the expense of the Admiral and officers now in command of the South Atlantic Blockading Squadron. On the contrary, in the whole discussion, properly reviewed, the friends of the officers now commanding will find an ample explanation of the reasons which have operated for the disappointment of public expectation in regard to the attack upon Charleston. The fault is herein traced to its true source, and is found to rest in the inherent defects of the Monitors, and not in any incapacity on the part of their present commanders.

That portion of the volume relating to city and state politics, had for its object to promote the election of national and upright men, irrespective of person or party, to fill the chief offices of both City and State. Since the original appearance of these papers in the *Herald*, two elections have been held; and some friends of Private Miles are partial enough to believe that his songs may have had some little influence on the public opinion which shaped their results. The true explanation of the political revolution is too obvious, however, to leave any ground for vanity of this kind. The recent elections, not only through all the loyal States, but in all the States of the Confederacy, have shown certain distinctive characteristics:—a determination of the people to put down extremists of all colors: an utter distrust on the popular part of all old leaders, who fall under the title of "professional politicians;" and a popular resolve to place new men of good personal character in the seats of those who have held office heretofore without establishing any claim to other than official respect.

In the last part of the volume—that treating of presidential politics, the national vote and the army vote to be cast next year—Private O'Reilly has aspired in his songs to little more than a voicing forth of one strong current of opinion which he seems to have observed throughout the army. He is the *claqueur* of no candidate, and would, apparently, as soon vote—so far as personal grounds are concerned—for any one as for any other of the high officers or statesmen who are named by him as possible recipients of the army suffrage. It appears his aim in this matter to fix public attention on the necessity, or at least the expediency, of consulting the preferences and loyal instincts of our soldiers in the field, before determining upon whom shall be placed the mantle of nomination for the chief magistracy of the Union. Camps, in their own queer way, are places of very thorough national instruction. Regiments of men from all quarters of the loyal states are aggregated and mixed together in the larger organizations of our armies. They march, fight, and sleep under the same banner. No matter what their former habits or station in life, the same food is served out to all. Equal promotion awaits their merit; and if struck down by weapons or disease, they lie side by side in one general hospital, their attendance the same, and their nursing as affectionate. Falling on the battle-field they have common graves, and living they will have a common destiny. They are not hackneyed in the ways, nor corrupted by the habits of the "professional politician." National from the very necessities of their position, and eager beyond all others to secure a just and honorable Peace, which will remit them to their homes and happy firesides in a restored and vindicated Union—the wishes of the army in the approaching Presidential contest are most certainly entitled to some deference. No claim is advanced in behalf of this volume to an exclusive or perfect mirroring in its pages of the army mind. In every army there are different currents of opinion, but all with their tides in one general direction; and this hasty volume is but a chronicle of the currents which have flowed, and the general drift they have taken, under the view of one very humble soldier.

THE EDITOR.

NEW YORK, *December 5th*, 1863.

PRIVATE MILES O'REILLY.

CHAPTER I.

THE IRON-CLADS. DU PONT'S ATTACK ON SUMTER.

IN CAMP, FOLLY ISLAND, S. C., April 25, 1863.

MY DEAR N: Our friend, Major Wright, showed me one paragraph of your letter to him, in which you referred, apparently with surprise, to the fact that the attack on Charleston by the iron-clads should have been discontinued "when so few casualties had occurred." This is so obvious a reflection, on the first hasty view of the affair, and one so radically unjust when we look calmly at the facts, that, in Major Wright's absence (he has gone down the posts along the Florida coast on a tour of inspection) I will venture to occupy your time a few moments on the subject.

In ordinary warfare the amount of casualties will give a fair idea of the strength of the resistance and the power and persistency of the attack. With wooden vessels, your remark, as previously quoted—and I know it to be an all but universal one—would apply with truth; and it is because we have all become so accustomed to measure battles on land or sea by the amount of slaughter and maiming inflicted, that we are apt to err in judging an utterly uncommon and unprecedented battle by the ordinary or common standard. Let me also add that this standard is both a vulgar and false one. McClellan's victory at Yorktown was a bloodless one, but, nevertheless, a triumph of the highest importance in its results. Of Halleck's siege and capture of Corinth, the same may be said—that victory, although a bloodless one, having thrown open the doors of the entire South-West to the conquering advance of our armies.

And now, let me submit to you, more in detail,

some few hasty reflections on the subject of the recent operations for the capture of Charleston:—

1. It is to be borne in mind that this (so far as the navy was concerned) was purely an experiment as to the possibility of taking a city by machinery. The Monitors might be called blood-saving instruments, with this penalty attached to them: that whenever the loss of life should begin, it would involve the almost certain destruction of every man on board. The number of men in the whole iron-clad squadron was less than a regiment; and these few hundred men, rushing against thirty or forty thousand behind powerful fortifications, were to have no other part in the fight than to supply the necessary power for working the machines. If Charleston were to fall, it was by machinery; and the moment the experiment was tested to the point of proving that the machines were inadequate to their work, it was wisdom to withdraw them, and would have been dangerous foolhardiness to have held them longer exposed.

2. The experiment was fully prosecuted up to this point, with a magnificence of gallantry before which every generous and just spectator, not directly involved in the attack, must have bowed in reverence. The machines were untried, and the conflict was the

first practical test we have ever had of the power of the new kinds of ordnance and ordnance material employed against them. I refer to the Blakely and Whitworth English guns, firing bolts and steel-pointed shot. The warfare was almost as new to Admiral Du Pont and his Captains as it would have been to you or myself—new kinds of projectiles raining on them from above; vast torpedoes known to be underneath their keels, and every channel of entrance blocked up with triple rows of torpedo-armed obstructions.

3. After less than an hour's conflict, five out of the eight Monitors were disabled—the Keokuk sinking. Behind the forts, calmly waiting their opportunity, lay three of the enemy's iron-clads in plain view: vessels not able in fair fight to live an hour before one of our Monitors; but held in readiness to cruise out and capture any Monitor disabled by the artillery practice of the forts and batteries. This should not be let out of sight.

4. With two or three of our vessels of this kind disabled, captured, repaired, and in the enemy's service, what force would it require to maintain the blockade of Charleston? Wooden vessels—our gunboats and steam-sloops—would be useless; and our

iron vessels could not live outside of Charleston bar in rough weather. Nor, even if they could, unless we had enough of them to cross-fire over every inch of the mouth of the harbor permanently, could a blockade be maintained against the fast clipper steamers built as blockade-runners in English ship-yards. In a word, the enemy, with a single Monitor of ours, could drive every wooden boat from the blockade: and the blockade would thus practically be raised.

5. Could we afford to have Charleston a free port—the greatest free port in the world, when viewed as the only outlet and inlet for the commerce of eight millions of people; with arms and all other requisites pouring into it unmolested, and cotton, tobacco, naval stores, and so forth, pouring out? Would not such an event of necessity—a moral and political necessity — compel France, and perhaps other wavering foreign Powers, to acknowledge the Confederacy? Are we in a position lightly to hazard these consequences?

6. Bear in mind that the weakness of the Monitor-turrets was increasing in geometrical ratio under the force of each concussion. Each bolt started, each plate cracked, each stancheon bent by the first ball,

left weaker protection against the second; and the second transmitted this deterioration, increased by its own impact, to the third. Thus onward--the element of the calculation being that three hundred guns, worked with every advantage of space and fixity, were arrayed against thirty-two guns cramped up in delicate machines, and requiring to be fired just at the exact right moment of turretal rotation.

7. Fort Sumter itself, we should not forget, was but the fire-focus of two long, converging lines of forts and batteries; and while, for aggressive purposes, and from its position, its armament was more to be dreaded than that of any other work,—the fort itself, being built of masonry, fully exposed to fire, was the most pregnable point in the harbor. Nor would its fall have terminated the contest, nor given any further ease to the iron-clads, than the withdrawal of so many guns from against them. Their work would still lie before them, in silencing the other forts and removing the triple line of powerful and cunningly devised obstructions.

The foregoing, my dear N——, are only a few of the most prominent suggestions to be used in forming a right estimate of the struggle. Busy and overworked as I am, this explanation has appeared necessary to my conscience as a point of duty: insomuch that I could not rest until my very utmost was done to let you see this affair from the standpoint of a deeply interested spectator, who had given some thought and observation to the problem, and who certainly has no other interest in this matter than to see that no injustice is done to brave, true patriots whom he honors—honors with his whole heart and soul.

How I should have felt if in the Weehawken, commanded by John Rodgers, who had the post of honor in the van, I do not know; but suppose that pride and the busy sense of duty and responsibility would have held me firm to my work. Only a spectator, however, with no immediate cares to distract my attention, I am not ashamed to say that I trembled like a leaf for the gallant souls on board the Weehawken, when she first steamed into the hell-made-visible fronting and around Fort Sumter.

The chief officers, as you know, who took part in this fight were Admiral Du Pont, Commodore Turner, Fleet Captain Ramon Rodgers, Dupont's chief of staff; and Commanders John Rodgers, Drayton of

South Carolina, brother to General Drayton of the Confederate army; George W. Rodgers, Daniel Ammen, Downs, Fairfax, Worden, who commanded the original Monitor in her fight with the Merrimac in Hampton Roads; and Rhind who, with rash gallantry, ran his vessel, the Keokuk, right under the walls of Fort Sumter, in which position she was so badly riddled and ripped up with bolts and percussion shells, that she sank next morning, despite all efforts to keep her afloat and send her down for repairs to Port Royal. I record these names because it gives me pleasure to write them. It is with names such as these that the future crown of the Republic will be most brightly jewelled.

And here let me give you a few verses, on the subject of the iron-clads, which are said to have been picked up in a bottle on the shore of Seabrooke Island by a soldier named Miles O'Reilly—a youthful warrior of Italian extraction—belonging to the 47th New York, but now detached as an orderly at the Headquarters of Brigadier-General Thos. G. Stevenson, Commanding United States troops around Edisto Inlet. As several of the Monitors are lying in the Edisto, some think, from intrinsic evidence, that the verses must have been written on board one of them by some officer acquainted with their demerits; but who, fearing the wrath of the higher powers, could not publish them in regular form, and was therefore obliged to launch his only edition in a sealed bottle over the side of his ship.

Our friend Commander George W. Rodgers is strong in this belief; and his suspicions as to the authorship are almost equally divided between Commanders Beaumont, Ammen and Downs, with the heaviest balance of suspicion against the first named of these officers. Others, who are not in the Navy, think that the lines are the work of Private M. O'Reilly's own brain, the stanzas being revised and put into good English by a certain Chaplain Hudson of the Volunteer Engineers, who has a taste for literature, and is known to be "in cohoot" with O'Reilly, who has become quite famous in a small way throughout the Department for comic songs and impromptu verses about the incidents of the day. This latter class are of opinion that there "never was no bottle at all,"—much as the ungrateful Betsy once insulted Mrs. Sairey Gamp by saying, that "there never was no such a person as Mrs. Harris!" Be these things as they may, the lines, if containing little poetry, are as full of sense as an egg is full of meat;

and whether written by Beaumont, Ammen, Downs, Hudson or Private O'Reilly, they reveal certain truths which the authorities at Washington should by no means overlook.

AN IDYL OF THE IRON-CLADS.

CONSIDERABLY AFTER MR. EMERSON'S "BRAHMA."

[*Lines picked up in a bottle by Private Miles O'Reilly.*]

If the torpedoer's torpedes
 Knock the torpedoed high in air,
Won't Uncle Gideon, as he reads,
 Look solemn through his silvery hair!

Vague or forgot the navy seems
 To Gideon slumbrous in the dark,
Stroking his beard in happy dreams,
 Or studying plans from Noah's ark.

Vainly we labor hard and long
 To paint the errors of the ships,
Entranced by Stimers' syren song,
 His judgment lieth in eclipse.

Rifles and smooth-bores are the same,
 He cares not for a turret jammed;
Prompt from himself to turn all blame,
 He muttereth mildly "That be——rammed!"

The strong men of the navy pine,
  But pines not that forsaken crew
Of those who, in the contract line,
  Proclaim "what Monitors can do."

We hoist our bottoms from the sea
  To show why slow and wild we steered,
Coated with polyps dull as he
  And grasses lengthy as his beard;—

But this in him no terror breeds
  Who muttereth—"Spite of all the shocks
Of storms, and battles, and torpedes
  I must be guided by my Fox!

"Though foul their bottoms as the heart
  Of Toucey or Fernando Wood,
Though plates are cracked and stancheons start
  And every pilot-house runs blood;

"Although the pendent grasses drop
  On rocks a dozen fathoms down,
Though on their sides the oyster crop
  Be large enough to feed a town;

"Though turrets jam and won't revolve,
  Though guns kick off the track within,
It still is Gideon's grim resolve,
  On Ericsson his faith to pin.

"And woe to him who on his cuff
  Weareth gold lace, or round his cap,
If, by expostulations rough,
  He waketh Gideon from his nap!"

Thus Gideon muttered, half awake,
  Thinking the iron-clads a bore,
Then turning, a fresh snooze to take,
  Fox entering heard the great man snore.

Before concluding this letter—hastily written, but containing points, it seems to me, which you might do the country a service by bringing to the notice of Mr. Lincoln—let me call attention to the manifest impolicy of further increasing our fleet of Monitor built iron-clads. These vessels, admirable perhaps for attacking fortified places along our coasts—although they have been badly repulsed at Forts McAlister and Sumter—are manifestly unfit to cross the ocean, except when a guaranty-deed of "dead calm" shall have been obtained from the Clerk of the Weather; and are just as manifestly unfit for human beings to live in for any length of time. Besides, it is clear, that, with the reduction of Charleston and Mobile, all the work for which this class of vessels is peculiarly fitted will have been accomplished.

I know it is said that they could be used as floating batteries with which to defend our harbors; but ask the men best competent to judge of their capacities as against vessels like the Warrior, Guerrière, La Gloire, etc., and this illusion will be dissipated. In the judgment of men who have commanded these little, low-lying, two-gun, slow sailing, floating batteries, one of the vast iron-clad frigates of France or England could receive the fire of any two of them—eight or ten guns at most—and then run right over them, the vast ploughs which such frigates carry in front, beneath the water, ripping the whole lower skin of the Monitor-hulls to pieces, and their tall prows moving on undisturbed over the little circular towers and pilot-houses, which would go down in eddying whirlpools beneath their irresistible weight and impetus.

Believe me, my dear N——, that we need iron-clad frigates; and fast vessels to fight fast vessels. There is not one of our grass-grown Monitors to-day that can make, to save her life, even in tideless water, over five miles an hour, if so much; while the mailed frigates of France and England make from seven to eleven and a half. In this respect also, the Roanoke is a failure, only making six knots per hour; and our only safeguard against invasion, and our only means of aggression in case of a foreign war, must be looked for in such vessels as Mr. Webb, of New York, is now constructing.

Cannot the Navy Department be made to realize these obvious facts? Cannot Mr. Assistant Secretary Fox—whose abilities and zeal are highly spoken of by many who are in the best position to judge—cannot he be brought to comprehend that all vessels-of-war must be in their nature a compromise between the best shape and construction for the immediate purposes of battle—occurring, mayhap, once in several years; and the necessity for having such accommodations, ventilation, comforts, etc., as will preserve the health of the men and officers forming the respective crews? These questions are asked by every unprejudiced naval officer at this station; and it is important that the matter should receive the prompt attention of all who are interested in city property along the Atlantic and Pacific seaboards.

CHAPTER II.

THE ARREST OF PRIVATE MILES.

MORRIS ISLAND, S. C., August 29, 1863.

MY DEAR HUDSON: A most ridiculous incident has occurred here, which nevertheless threatened, but for the prompt measures adopted by Lieutenant-Colonel J. F. Hall, Provost Marshal General, to have resulted, perhaps, in a weakening of the strong regard which has heretofore subsisted between our land and naval forces. The facts are as follows:—

There is in one of the New York regiments an odd character named Miles O'Reilly, who has frequently relieved the monotony of camp life by scribbling songs on all sorts of subjects, and writing librettos for the various "minstrel companies," got up in imitation of George Christy's, at different posts of the Department during periods of repose.

His last effort was a song, advising Admiral Dahlgren to go home, and warmly espousing the interests of Admiral Du Pont and the former commanders of the iron-clads, in whose behalf his affections seem warmly enlisted, he having served for some months as a volunteer marine on board the Pawnee, Wabash, Ironsides, Paul Jones, and other vessels of the South Atlantic Blockading Squadron.

These verses he managed in some mysterious manner to have printed in regular street ballad form, either on the press of Mr. J. H. Sears, at Hilton Head; or, more probably, in the office of General Saxton's *Free South*, at Beaufort. At any rate he got them printed, and they soon were in the hands of nearly every soldier—the men singing them with intense and uproarious relish to an old Irish air, slightly altered—the Shan Van Voght, which Private O'Reilly taught them.

At last the song attracted the attention of some naval officers who were ashore on a visit to Col. J. W. Turner, "a corn-fed boy from Illinoy," and Col. J. J. Elwell, Chief Quartermaster of the Department; and they, having mentioned the matter to some army associates, Col. J. F. Hall was very quickly on the track of the author, and had no difficulty in tracing the squib to O'Reilly, who was at once placed in confinement, with a sixty-four pound shot at each heel, to aid, perhaps, in preventing any further Pegasinian or Olympian flights. He takes his punishment good-humoredly; compares himself to Galileo, "an ould cock that was tortured for telling the thruth;" and is at present busily writing an appeal in verse to Secretary Stanton. In order that you may be able to judge of the enormity of the breach of discipline of which O'Reilly has been guilty, I transmit herewith a printed copy of his song:—

THE ARMY TO THE IRON-CLADS.

(*With an accompaniment of bombshells, Greek fire, and two hundred pounder rifled shots.*)

Och! Admiral Dahlgreen,
It is aisy to be seen
That ashore so long you've been
  You can never toe the mark;

Of your ships you seem as chary
As my little black-eyed Mary
Of her silver-winged canary
   Or her crockery Noah's ark.

'Tis no harm, you seem to think,
That upon desthruction's brink—
He is not the boy to shrink–
   Our gallant Gillmore stands;
Houlding hard his threatened lines,
Pushin' far his saps and mines,
While you—knowin' his designs—
   Idly sit with folded hands.

Give us back our own Du Pont!
Ramon Rodgers, too, we want,
Send the say-dogs to the front
   Who have fought the fight before;
John Rodgers, Dhrayton, Rhind,
Ammen—grim, but always kind—
Aye, and Worden, though half blind,
   Let us have their lead once more!

Woe's me! George Rodgers lies,
Wid dimmed and dhreamless eyes,
He has airly won the prize
   Of the sthriped and starry shroud;—
While some fought shy away
He pushed far into the fray,
As if ayger thus to say,
   "All the lads have not been cowed!"

Staunch Fairfax and thrue Downs,
Born layguerers of towns!
"No chance here of laurel crowns,"
Thus it seems I hear you sighin';
"'Twas not always so," you say,
"When Du Pont in every fray
Led the line and cleared the way,
Wid his broad blue pennon flyin'."

Och! Gideon, King of men!
Take Dahlgreen home again,
And let Fulton's glowin' pen
All his high achavements blazon—
For Fulton, Gideon mine!
Can paint pictures, line by line,
All of that precise design
You and Fox delight to gaze on.

Dear Uncle Gideon, oh!
Let Dahlgreen homeward go!
He's a shmart man, as we know,
And the guns he makes are sthriking;
Keep him always on the make,
Do, Gid, for pity's sake;
But the warrior lead to take,
Let us have Du Pont, the Viking!

What disposition will eventually be make of private Miles O'Reilly, who has twice risen to sergeant and twice been "sot back" for eccentric breaches of discipline, it would be hard to guess. Lieutenant Colonel E. W. Smith, General Gillmore's Assistant Adjutant General, is at a loss to know under what article of war the crime of song-writing can be punished. Officers of a naturally severe cast of countenance will also be required to avoid unseemly laughter during the sessions of the court. Besides, there is a strong feeling, I regret to say, among all the men and many of the subordinate officers in O'Reilly's favor: and while many, wearing the double rows of buttons, declare he should be severely dealt with, very nearly all the single-breasted coats, with or without shoulder-straps, think it would do no injury to postpone his trial until after an article of war against song writing shall have been added to those now in force by the next Congress.

It is rumored that copies of the song in question have permeated the navy, and that nearly all the wardroom messes have under discussion the propriety of signing a petition for O'Reilly's release. Meantime it is difficult, even for Colonel Hall, to enforce that rigorous treatment of the prisoner which he is thought to deserve, as the soldiers, to a man, believe he is unfairly punished; and the provost guard have twice been found smuggling in dainties to him—his prescribed and proper daily diet being eighteen ounces of bread with two quarts of cold water. General A. H. Terry, we hear, offers to release the prisoner if he will disclose the name of the printer of his incendiary song. This offer O'Reilly indignantly spurns, saying he "never sould the pass in his life, nor never will;" and winds up by asking do they take him for a "soup kitchen convert," or one of "Lord Clarendon's Jimmy O'Briens." These phrases are all Greek to us down here, even in this region of Greek fire; but mayhap "Irish Tom," opposite the Custom House, may be able to translate them into English.

Before quitting this subject, let me say that the attempts made in certain quarters to exalt the present achievements of the South Atlantic Blockading Squadron, at the expense of its late commander, Admiral Du Pont, will have an effect rather the reverse of that intended by those who are engaged in this paltry business. No one whose authority in such matters is of any weight, thinks of blaming Admiral Dahlgren for the extreme caution he has thus far displayed in exposing his iron-clads to fire. He ranks second to no officer in the navy as a commander of gallantry and nerve. But the tools in his hands are utterly inadequate to the work they are expected to accomplish; and, in taking him out of the Ordnance Bureau of the Navy, in which his services have been invaluable for the last fifteen or twenty years, and placing him suddenly, and with but little actual sea-experience, in command of so vast an undertaking as this of Charleston,—it is felt that Secretary Welles has committed his favorite error of placing the right man in the wrong place, and imposing upon Dahlgren a task under which he must most certainly break down.

It is well understood by all here that, with the destruction of Fort Sumter and the capture of Forts Wagner and Gregg, the main business of the land forces under General Gillmore will have been accomplished. Indeed, this is all General Gillmore bargained to do when making those representations which resulted in his appointment to the command. Nothing will then remain for him but to shell Charleston, at long range, from Cumming's Point; and here, *en parenthèse*, let me remark that the accident to the three hundred pounder Parrott gun does not, as was at first supposed, at all disable that gun. The injury was received from the untimely bursting of a shell, just as it was passing out of the bore. This accident blew off the muzzleband; but the remainder of the piece is uninjured, and in as good condition as ever for practical work.

And now to return to the iron-clad matter, of which I set out to speak. It is not generally known, but is nevertheless true, that Admiral Dahlgren is, and has been for the last ten days, confined to his bed by sickness, or has only been able to crawl on deck or into the pilot-house on critical occasions. The abominable atmosphere of the iron-clads has taken hold of his system, and nothing but his high resolution, and the necessity he is under of vindicating the action of the Navy Department, which placed him in command, can long sustain him under his present debility. So fixed is his determination to go through with his work, however, that he has not in any of his dispatches to the Department even referred to his ill-health; and it is only by private letters from sympathizing friends that the North can hear of his condition. He doubtless feels that, under the peculiar circumstances attending Du Pont's removal, a more than common anxiety must be felt by the Navy Department for the exertions to the uttermost of the officer who has succeeded the victor of Port

Royal, and the thrice gallant first assailer of Fort Sumter.

In Du Pont's attack, it must be remembered, all the iron-clads ran up to within eight hundred yards of the then uninjured fort,—Captain Rhind, in the ill-fated Keokuk, running in to within four hundred yards, and fighting desperately for thirty minutes at that distance, only withdrawing under orders, and at a moment when his vessel was a sinking ruin;—while in the present operations, assisted by Gillmore's powerful land batteries, Admiral Dahlgren, reserving his vessels for work farther up the roadstead, has wisely held them not closer than two thousand yards to Fort Sumter, while that work was still in a condition to reply effectively to his fire—two thousand yards being very nearly the extreme effective range of his fifteen-inch smooth bores.

Under these circumstances, Du Pont may possibly be condemned for rashness, or Dahlgren commended for prudence; but it is obviously worse than absurd to indulge in any sneers or indirect innuendoes or cavils against Du Pont's attack as if it had lacked in gallantry. The Old Viking of the South Atlantic blockading squadron is the last man in the world among his peers—men personally acquainted with him and professionally competent to judge him —to whom such a charge will stick. No braver or more intelligent officers ever lived than his subordinate iron-clad commanders—John Rodgers, Rhind, Drayton, Fairfax, Ammen, Downs, Worden, Turner, and the lamented George W. Rodgers, who lost his life, as you are aware, while running his vessel in to within one hundred and fifty yards of Fort Wagner.

There is one point, however, in Admiral Dahlgren's course which excites a good deal of laughing commentary among our army officers. It is this:—On the 23d inst. Colonel John W. Turner, the "corn fed boy from Illinoy," who is General Gillmore's chief of staff and of artillery, ceases fire against Fort Sumter, on the ground that it is an inoffensive ruin, which could be still more completely made a pile of broken brick and powdered mortar by further fire; but which could not, by any amount of fire, be rendered more completely harmless as against the iron-clads than in its then condition. The day after this, on the 24th inst., the iron-clads, idle or only firing at long range during the previous ten days against this particular fort, announced their intention of making "an attack in force on the work," and our army friends are jocosely anticipating that the New York papers will some day tell you of the "Surrender of Fort Sumter to the iron-clads" in startling capitals,—the announcement adding that on such a day so many hundred marines and seamen "landed on the ruined ramparts, and, gallantly climbing over the shattered arches and parades, hoisted the Stars and Stripes and took possession of the work in the name of the navy—another glorious victory to the—marines!" The western officers in particular are strong in this belief. They say they saw the same thing done at Island No. Ten; and on this point, but in connexion with the siege of Vicksburg, they tell a story which is rather hard upon the "bummers," or mortar schooners and gunboats, employed in the reduction of that place.

They say that Lieutenant-General Pemberton once asked Grant for a truce to bury his dead outside the works. This was while Grant was attacking from the land circumvallation, while the naval forces were throwing shells high up in the air to fall down over the bluffs into the devoted city. Grant answered that he had no objection, but would require some hours to consult with Admiral Porter, in order to have the navy cease firing as well as the land forces.

"O, if that be your only cause for wishing delay, never mind it," was the prompt answer of the rebel negotiator. "If your land batteries on a level with us will only stop, the bummers and gunboats may keep firing at the moon until the day of Judgment." The same Western officers further allege that the same principle which would justify the navy in claiming Fort Sumter as their prize, was amply illustrated in the flaming bulletins which announced the capture of the Haines Bluff batteries, after they had been evacuated under the stress put upon them through General Sherman's corps, by the Mississippi flotilla.

These remarks, I am fully aware, are extremely ill-natured, and may even appear frivolous to men who cannot understand that honor is the highest prize for which our soldiers and sailors are contending. But beyond doubt there cannot be so much smoke without fire; and it is for the best interests of both branches of the service that each should know the alleged points of grievance between them. The navy has such an abundance of laurels, that none of its true friends—and I claim to be one of its truest—could wish to deprive the army of a single twig or leaf that is justly due to it.

As for other matters, the wisest here think that

Admiral Dahlgren's caution in the opening of the Charleston conflict will be abundantly justified when the nature of the work yet to be accomplished is understood by the public. Fort Sumter—weakest for defence, most powerful for the offensive—is now happily eliminated from the problem which the iron-clads have yet to solve. But Forts Moultrie and Johnson, Battery Bee, Battery Beauregard, Castle Pinckney and Fort Ripley, still remain to be settled with; and in the attack upon these General Gillmore can give but little assistance. Against Fort Moultrie, the strongest defensive work in the harbor, he can do almost nothing. Fort Johnson is on the extreme left of Beauregard's line of defences, stretching across James Island from the harbor line to Secessionville. To attack this line in general would require a force more than treble that now at Gen. Gillmore's disposal; and his only means of advancing under cover against the fort, would be to start trenches, zigzags and parallels from where the Swamp Angel Battery is now located, along the narrow strip of hard sand-shore which lies between the swamps and the harbor-line. This strip of hard sand would offer very nearly the same obstacle to trenching that would be offered by the pavements and sub-soil of

Broadway; and, exhausted as his men are by the labors they have already performed, and the malarial cachexia which has reduced their systems, it is doubtful if his whole force, applied to the spade and pick for the next three months, would suffice to advance a mine under the walls of Fort Johnson. Most probably—indeed almost certainly—Gen. Gillmore, on obtaining possession of Cummings' Point, will open at long range with his three, two, and one hundred pounder Parrots against Charleston city, keeping his troops in a state of tranquil amusement, while watching the effects of Greek fire amongst the buildings of Meeting and King streets; and generously admiring the splendid exertions of courage, labor, and science by which his confrères of the navy propose to remove the various lines of torpedo-armed obstructions now blocking up Charleston harbor.

CHAPTER III.

O'REILLY'S PETITION TO MR. STANTON.

IN CAMP, MORRIS ISLAND, S. C., Aug. 20, 1863.

I REGRET to have to inform you that the publication in your columns of the song written by Private Miles O'Reilly of the 47th regiment New York Volunteers, has only led to the still severer treatment of that imprisoned bard. Had I foreseen, when sending you the song for your private amusement, that it could by any possibility have occurred to you to put it on record in the *N. Y. Herald*, my sincere sympathy for the prisoner would have led me to caution you against the adoption of such a course. Now that the thing has become matter of public notoriety, General A. H. Terry, commanding the Post, has nothing for it but to let O'Reilly suffer the penalty of his offence; nor could General Gillmore, with propriety or delicacy, interpose the prerogative of his clemency in regard to a crime of which the particulars have been so widely bruited. The balls, therefore, must remain on poor Miles for some time, and all the rigors of his confinement have been, if anything, increased. He is now attended by Chaplain Hudson, of the New York Volunteer Engineers, formerly well known in your city as a minister of the Gospel, and lecturer on the beauties of Shakspeare. Between Miles and the chaplain a very tender sentiment of esteem is said to have been developed; and it was upon Mr. Hudson's intercession that General Gillmore finally consented to forward O'Reilly's petition (of which I spoke in my last) to the Secretary of War. The first song having been unfortunately published, it can do no further injury to let the petitioner's defence of himself, see the light.

What disposition will be made of it by Mr. Stanton, all down here are at a loss to imagine. Some think that, if the President's attention could be called to the case, his own proclivity to a joke might make him look with leniency on the luckless rhymer of Morris Island. The petition reads as follows, but to appreciate its true pathos and humor one should hear O'Reilly sing it himself. His recitative of the parts in parenthesis has never been surpassed:—

MEMORIAL OF PRIVATE MILES O'REILLY, NOW AN ONLUCKY PRISONER IN THE GUARDHOUSE.

To His Excellency the Right Hon. EDWIN M. STANTON, Esq., and all others whom it may concern:—

AIR—"*The Fine Ould English Gentleman.*"

I'll sing to you a navy song
  Made by a soldier's pate,
Of a galliant, grim ould Admiral,
  Whom iron jobbers hate—
Because he couldn't, or didn't, or wouldn't
  Some fibs in their favor state:
For which he has several big black marks
(Wid no end of notes of disadmiration, an' great big, ugly criss crasses forninst his name),
  On Uncle Gideon's slate—
This galliant, grim ould Admiral,
  Wan of the oulden time!

'Twas he who, whin our skies wor dark,
  Nigh twinty months ago,
Let rifts of daylight through the clouds
  In glorious lusthre flow;
"The fight is done! Port Royal won!"
  Och, didn't the counthry crow,
An' didn't ould Uncle Gideon

(Aye, and all the administhration organs, big and little, from Colonel Forney's "Philadelphia Fibber" down to Horace Greeley's very weakly "Thribune")

  Of the mighty vic'thry blow,
An' praise the grim ould Admiral,
  As "wan of the rale ould time?"

An' 'twas him that tuk the iron-clads
  Last spring aginst Fort Sumther;
And 'twas him that, at seven or eight hundhred yards,
  Wid his fifteen-inchers bumped her;
And 'twas Rhind, wid his two big rifled guns
  That at half the distance thumped her—
While the present Admiral stands off

(At the convaynient perspective distance of two thousand yards or thereabouts, until even the poor forsook ruin of a place seems to grow weary of waitin' for him),

  An' don't, by a long shot, come t' her
So near as the grim ould Admiral,
  Who is wan of the oulden time!

But now this great ould Admiral
Is laid upon the shelf,
Like a broken chaney taypot
Or a useless piece of delf,
Because he couldn't, or didn't, or wouldn't,
(An' for this, more power to himself!)
Chime in wid them iron-clad jobbers

(Who are down on their bare knees, every mother's son of them, night, noon and mornin', prayin' Heaven or the other place for long life and success to Du Pont's inimies)

In their schaimes for acquirin' pelf—
This honest an' thrue ould Admiral,
This type of the bygone time!

An' because on the side of this Admiral,
I used both me tongue an' me pen,
I am now chained up like a un-u-i-corn
In the Provost-Marshal's den,
Wid nothin' but hard tack an' wather—
If it worn't for the Provost's men
Who shmuggle me in, God bless the boys!

(On the sly, do you see, an' just by way of keepin' me sperrits up, an' purventin' me leg-ornamints from takin' the skin off my ankles too much),

Some whiskey, now an' agen,
Which I dhrink to the great ould Admiral,
Whom I knew in the bygone time.

Och! Stanton, our great God of War,
My condition in pity see,
An' if you have got any bowels to melt
Let your bowels be melted for me;—
For I come of the daycintest people
In the beautiful town of Thralee,
Where praties an' whishkey is plenty,
(An' divil resayve the provost marshal we have there, at all at all, though we have the "peelers"—bad 'cess to 'em—who is worse, if such a thing wor possible)—
And they bow both heart an' knee
To men like the grim ould Admiral—
A type of the oulden time!

God be good to you, Misther Stanton,
An' look kindly on me case;
An' to the man wid Methusaleh's beard
An' the pathriarchal face
(I mane ould Uncle GideonWelles),
Just ax him to show me grace,
For which I will, as in duty bound,
If he gets me out of this place—
Do for him an' for you all that ever I can
(Votin' airly and votin' often for yez both, or for aither of you, if yez ever chance to be candydates in any dishtrick or county where I can get widin ten rods of the ballot box,
An' now my name I thrace—
Miles O'Reilly, who wrote of the Admiral,
An' is havin' a hard ould time!

Of course such a document as the foregoing can hardly hope to receive grave or serious attention at the War Department, nor is it at all likely that Mr. Stanton will order O'Reilly's irons to be taken off in consequence of this rhythmical prayer. The commanding officer of the Forty-seventh regiment is now absent on leave, and is believed to be staying at his home in your city. The greatest anxiety to have him return, so that he may be present at the trial, is manifested by the prisoner, who relies largely upon his evidence as to his (O'Reilly's) general good conduct as a soldier.

Dr. Marsh, the Chief Inspector of the Sanitary Commission, visits the guard-house frequently, and does all that he can for the unhappy culprit, in whom so much interest is felt. It is due also to Surgeon J. J. Craven, Medical Purveyor, to say that he has been unremitting in his attentions; as has also been Surgeon Dibble, of the Sixth Connecticut Volunteers, who declares it to be his opinion, after close examination, that this is what Mr. James T. Brady, of your city, would call a case of "moral insanity;" and that the prisoner having a monomania for writing verses, should not be held responsible before a military tribunal. This plea, however, is not accepted; and, as things look now, the balls and chains will not be taken off O'Reilly until further orders. Lieut.-Colonel J. F. Hall, Provost Marshal General, is now at the North, and it is believed that he will take Secretary Stanton's orders in the case before returning.

And now a word to the correspondent of a paper published in Baltimore, who is well known to write under the immediate inspiration of the iron-clad interest, and who has of late been laboring to prove that my former letters in reference to the Monitor question, have been a tissue of blunders and errors of statement written by one having no practical knowledge of his subject-matter—the strong inference from his own letter being (though modesty does not allow him to state the matter in open words), that he alone is the repository of all iron-clad information,—thus ignoring not only the present writer, a very small matter; but also Mr. Osbun, the chief iron-clad reporter of the *Herald*, who has sailed and served in the Monitors for many months, and who is painfully familiar with the sensations caused to men inside the pilot-house and turret by the concussions of shot striking and shell exploding against the exterior walls and on the deck.

For my inexperience in matters naval and military, I tender apologies to this correspondent. In newspaper controversies he will find me a mere neophyte; and, never having been in any position of command, my style unavoidably lacks that authoritative, not to say dogmatic and dictatorial tone so pleasantly conspicuous in all he writes.

His intimacy with all the iron-clad inventors and contractors, gives him an advantage over me in estimating the value of that class of ships; and if, as he seems to think, the object of such vessels be to secure the safety from hostile missiles of the three occupants of each pilot house, and the sixteen men forming the practical gun-crew in each turret, it may at once be admitted, that, as nearly as any human machinery can, they approximate perfection; and this more especially when at an average distance of two thousand yards from the enemy's ordnance.

But when Rhind took the Keokuk* within four hundred yards of Sumter, his ship was riddled and sunk; and when George W. Rodgers ran within one hundred and fifty yards of Wagner,† the penalty of his rash gallantry was paid with his life. The only unfortunate point in regard to the two thousand

---

* Not a "Monitor" exactly. † In the *Catskill*, a regular Monitor.

yards safety theory is this:—that the distance named converts the contest on both sides into very much of a sham battle, a sort of child's bargain—"You don't hurt me, and I won't hurt you."

When Worden first steamed up to Fort McAllister, on the Ogeechee, the men and officers thronged out on the ramparts of that small earthwork to see what an iron-clad was like. Worden himself directed one of his guns and burst a shell immediately over their heads, thereby killing Major Barstow, second in command under Colonel Anderson, and wounding several of the men. After this he opened a steady bombardment of the work, in which he was joined by three other Monitors, and the bombardment lasted several days and nights—with what result? Not another man of the garrison was killed. Not a gun was dismounted, and when the iron-clads, discomfited, steamed away, the fort was just as strong and substantially as uninjured as when the attack commenced!

Citing the case of the Atlanta—an ordinary commercial steamer, awkwardly and rapidly converted, with old railroad iron, into some semblance of a mail-clad war vessel—can furnish no parallel to the vast and fast iron-clad frigates and line-of-battle-ships now being built by the governments of France and England, and upon which all the ingenuity and resources of those two great countries are being lavished.—The Atlanta was caught in a corner, where her superior speed could give her no advantage, except for retreat. Her commander was a rash fool, who hazarded everything, and lost his vessel, rather than endure the mortification of turning tail in presence of certain distinguished ladies on board a river steamer—ladies, by the way, who had come down in no expectation of seeing one or more of our Monitors, but to see the Atlanta capture or destroy one small wooden gunboat which lay in Wassaw Sound. How the Weehawken and her consort happened to arrive so opportunely, is a point not yet explained in any navy dispatches that have been published.*

Accustomed to look for, and, when found, highly to appreciate, every grain of comfort in the bushels of official chaff almost daily poured out upon us in these disastrous times, I thank the correspondent in question for his assurance that "the Navy Department is not insensible to the fact, that iron-plated frigates are needed to meet and fight the same class of vessels on the high seas." With this point conceded, the controversy may well close,—its main object having

* Since explained in a letter from Admiral Du Pont, dated January 8th, 1864.

been to impress upon the country, that our Monitors are not all that we need, nor even any great part of what we need in the way of a National Navy. The second object has also been accomplished—not by these letters, indeed, but by the sure developments of time. The reputation of Admiral Du Pont, and of his gallant subordinate commanders, has been thoroughly rescued from the obloquy or suspicion, with which, in certain quarters, there appeared a disposition to cloud it. As for the reputation of General Hunter, also assailed, that too will take care of itself in the proper time and manner. Suffice it for the present that in all the military operations General Hunter undertook, or is blamed for having failed to undertake, he was governed by clear and peremptory orders; and that, many months before the first attack upon Fort Sumter, he in conjunction with Admiral Du Pont, submitted to those in higher authority precisely and identically the same plan of action, which has since to a qualified extent—all the extent he prophesied—proved successful under the magnificent engineering skill of General Gillmore, and the coöperation of the ironclads under their present Admiral.

CHAPTER IV.

MILES O'REILLY PARDONED.

WASHINGTON DISPATCH, *N. Y. Herald*, Oct. 1863.

WE are gratified to be able to announce that the President, always attentive to the cry of suffering and deserving soldiers, has granted a free pardon to Private Miles O'Reilly, Forty-seventh regiment New York Volunteers, now a prisoner on Morris Island, South Carolina. The President takes the view that O'Reilly's original offence was but "an innocent joke" in his own eyes, however contrary to the letter or spirit of the Revised Regulations for the Army. O'Reilly has been ordered North, and is expected here by the next steamer. Mr. Lincoln, in giving instructions to Colonel E. D. Townsend, Assistant Adjutant-General, for issuing the order of pardon, referred to the old proverb about "making the ballads of a nation, and allowing any one else to make the laws." It is believed that Miles will be confidentially employed at the White House in rendering into popular verse the stories and traditions of the great Northwest; and no doubt such a volume—the materials and anecdotes furnished by Mr. Lincoln, and the verses by the Bard of Green Erin—will be quite equal to anything in the same line since the days of Æsop's Fables, translated by the poet Gay.

It is said that the immediate impelling cause of this step on the part of the President—a very strong one in view of the stand taken with regard to Private O'Reilly by certain high authorities in the Navy Department—was a song brought to the notice of His Excellency by Captain Arthur M. Kinzie, of the Illinois Cavalry, a very deserving young officer, who, in the "halcyon days long ago," collected, drilled, and disciplined the first regiment of Colored Troops that had been raised in the United States since the days of General Andrew Jackson, who was of opinion —concurring therein with General George Washington—that colored men could stop a ball or fill a pit as well as better; and that the exclusive privilege of being killed or maimed in battle, or worked to death in the trenches, was not that kind of privilege for the exclusive right of which any great number of earnest and sensible white men could long contend. Capt. Kinzie, in the letter transmitting the following verses to the President, declared that they had been of the utmost value in reconciling the minds of the soldiery of the old 10th Army Corps to the experiment of the 1st South Carolina Volunteers. The verses were as follows; and although the author never declared himself, they were universally attributed through the Department of the South to Private Miles O'Reilly:—

SAMBO'S RIGHT TO BE KILT.

AIR—"*The Low-backed Car.*"

Some tell us 'tis a burnin' shame
  To make the naygers fight;
And that the thrade of bein' kilt
  Belongs but to the white:
But as for me, upon my sowl!
  So liberal are we here,
I'll let Sambo be murthered instead of myself,
  On every day in the year.
    On every day in the year, boys,
      And in every hour of the day;
    The right to be kilt I'll divide wid him,
      And divil a word I'll say.

In battle's wild commotion
  I shouldn't at all object
If Sambo's body should stop a ball
  That was comin' for me direct;
And the prod of a Southern bagnet,
  So ginerous are we here,
I'll resign, and let Sambo take it
  On every day in the year.
    On every day in the year, boys,
      And wid none o' your nasty pride,
    All my right in a Southern bagnet prod,
      Wid Sambo I'll divide!

The men who object to Sambo
  Should take his place and fight;
And it's betther to have a nayger's hue
  Than a liver that's wake and white.
Though Sambo's black as the ace of spades,
  His finger a thrigger can pull,
And his eye runs sthraight on the barrel-sights
  From undher its thatch of wool.
    So hear me all, boys darlin',
      Don't think I'm tippin' you chaff,
    The right to be kilt we'll divide wid him,
      And give him the largest half!

Whatever may be thought of the spirit animating this ditty—which certainly is extremely devoid of any philanthropic or humanitarian cant—the practical results of its popular diffusion redounded undoubtedly to the best interests of the service, "with a view to soup." The white soldiers of the Department began singing it round their camp-fires at night, and humming it to themselves on their sentry-beats. It made them regard the enlistment of the despised sons of Ham as rather a good joke at first; and next, as a joke containing some advantages to themselves. Very quickly they became reconciled to the experiment; and it was not long before they commenced to take in the movements and doings of their humble colored allies, that sort of half-ludicrous, half-pathetic interest which a jolly-hearted, full-grown elder brother takes in the first awkward attempts at manly usefulness that are made by "little Bub," who is some score of years his junior. This was General Hunter's object in all his orders and other measures relative to the organization of colored regiments. He urged the matter forward purely as a military measure, and without one syllable or thought of any "hnmanitarian proletarianism." Every black regiment in garrison would relieve a white regiment for service in the field. Every ball stopped by a black man would save the life of a white soldier. Besides, if the blacks are to have liberty, the strictness of military discipline is the best school in which their elevation to the plane of freedom can be conducted. It was Hunter's chief misfortune, and the greatest curse of his Department, that this purely military experiment was interfered with by a swarm of blackcoated, white-chokered, cotton-speculating, long-faced, philanthropy-preaching fanatics—the grand hierarch of whom appeared of opinion that "a white man, by severe moral restraint and constant attendance upon his (the grand hierarch's) preaching, might in time elevate himself to something very like an equality with an average buck-nigger just fresh from the plantations." For the presence of these civilians in the Department, General Hunter was not responsible; nor for the evil effects of their mischievous, and only mischievous, interference should he be blamed.

"That song," said the President, on hearing it read by Colonel Hay, "reminds me of what Deacon Stoddard, away down in Menard County, said one day, when a woman that was of suspected repute dropped a half eagle into the collection plate, after one of his charity sermons: 'I don't know where she gets it, nor how she earns it; but the money's good, and will do good. I wish she had some better way of getting it than she is thought to have; and that those who do get their money better, could be persuaded to make half as good a use of it.' I have no doubt, Hay, that O'Reilly, in whom you seem to take such an interest, might be a great deal better man than he is. But that song of his is both good and will do good. Let McManus step over to Colonel Townsend, and say that I want to see him." It was under these circumstances that Private Miles O'Reilly obtained his pardon.

CHAPTER V.

RETURN OF PRIVATE MILES O'REILLY.—HIS RECEPTION IN NEW YORK.

[*N. Y. Herald, Oct.*, 1863.

PRIVATE Miles O'Reilly, Forty-seventh regiment New York Volunteers, having been pardoned by the President for his breach of decorum in publishing songs relative to the joint naval and military operations against Charleston, came to this city in the Arago last week, having been given a thirty days' furlough by General Gillmore, at the end of which time he will proceed to Washington, and report to the President for special duty. Private O'Reilly was received by a large party of distinguished friends off Sandy Hook, on board the steam yacht of our excellent Port Surveyor, Mr. Rufus F. Andrews, who seems always ready to give both his vessel and his time to such festivities. Excellent speeches were made by General Daniel E. Sickles, Mr. James T. Brady, John Van Buren, Wm. E. Robinson, Commodore Joseph Hoxie, Judge Charles P. Daly, Daniel Devlin, and others; while Dr. Carmichael, Mr. John Savage, Mr. Stephen C. Massett, Mr. Barney Williams, and several celebrated songsters, amateur and professional, favored the company with patriotic and expressive melodies as the good vessel steamed up the Hudson on a brief pleasure trip.

Private O'Reilly is now staying at the residence of his cousin, Mr. James O'Reilly, quite a prominent democratic politician in the Sixteenth ward, who is at present employed in the City Inspector's Department. The military minstrel's health seems to have suffered somewhat from the rigors of his late confinement on Morris Island; but his spirits remain as high as ever, and his letter of versified thanks to

Mr. Lincoln is one of the most truly humorous things we have seen for many days. Of this production we can only give two verses—the first and second—O'Reilly saying that the balance (which treats liberally of the Cabinet difficulties and the "succession"), cannot appear until the President gives his consent to its publication,—Private Miles declaring that he has had his full share of punishment for publishing rhymes without authority, and that he is resolved never knowingly to be caught in the same bad scrape again. His letter to the President begins:—

Long life to you, Misther Lincoln!
  May you die both late an' aisy;
An' whin you lie wid the top of aich toe
  Turned up to the roots of a daisy,
May this be your epitaph, nately writ—
  "Though thraitors abused him vilely,
He was honest an' kindly, he loved a joke,
  An' he pardoned Miles O'Reilly!"

And for this same act while I've breath in me lungs
  Or a heart in me body beatin',
It's "long life to you, misther Lincoln!"
  That meself will keep repeatin':—
If you ain't the handsomest man in the world
  You've done handsome by me, an' highly;
And your name to poshterity will go down
  Arm in arm wid Miles O'Reilly!

The balance of this ditty we shall hope to present to our readers at an early day, it being extremely improbable that Mr. Lincoln will make himself a party to the desire of the Navy Department to have O'Reilly's light hid under a bushel. In the meantime the "bard of Morris Island," having dabbled a little in city politics before his enlistment, and having corresponded constantly, all the time he was away, with his cousin James, who is deep in all the mysteries of the Tammany and Mozart "machines," has got off the following "inside and partic'lar" view of the present condition of our local democratic wranglings, which may be read with amusement, and possibly with some instruction, by our fellow citizens of every stripe and hue. The "talk" in some of its paragraphs, like all other "oracular talk," may be dark to the outside heathen—the mere barbarians who have no other connexion with politics than to vote for the "machine candidates" and pay their taxes. But to the initiated, we are assured, every line and almost every syllable will convey a world of hard-headed and hard-hitting meaning. Private Miles says this last effusion of his genius is the "War Song of the Honist Dimmycrats of New York City Aginst the Chates;" and is anxious to have it sung before next election day either by Mr. Barney Williams or Mr. and Mrs. Florence, at the Academy of Music. He calls it—

THE BUST UP OF THE MACHINES.

AIR—*The Groves of Blarney.*

I.

Och, the coalition,
For a fair divishin
Of the city spoils, that was lately made;
It now proves a shwindle,
Which but sarves to kindle
Into fiercer fury min of every shade.
All the lads delightin',
In "payce" are fightin'
Like the divil himself aginst their new allies;
While aich "city rail-roadher"
Has around him an odher
Which even min wid noses the laste sinsitive do in their very heart of hearts most etarnally dispise!

II.

Yes, I tell you fairly,
Things looks mighty quarely
In the dimmycratic party of this daycint town;
The machines is busted
And all them that thrusted
In the reg'lar nominhins—Och, their tails is down!

It is fine insthruction
Just to see the ruction
That is made by Jim Brady an' McKeon too;
While there's Oliver Charlick,
Who is perfeck garlick
To Mister Pether B. Sweeny, Owny Brennan, Hughey Smith,
Jake Sharp, James B. Taylor, and to all that crew!

III.

There's the bould Fernandy,
Who was wanst our dandy—
He is now a mimber of the great "has beens"!
While fat Daycon Anson*
For revinge is prancin',
And is knockin' all the crockery into smithereens.
Here's the thrue John Kelly
Come to join the *melee*,
An' big Michael Connolly, stout as Brine O'Lynn;
Jump in and sthrip, boys!
To be whipped or whip, boys!
'Tis an ould-fashioned Donnybrook free fight, in which the best men win.

IV.

Here is War Horse Purdy,
Late so shpry an' sturdy,
Now so badly "Sweenied" that his teeth won't pass;
Take off his bridle,
Turn him out to idle,
You may cure his sthring halt wid a year of grass.

* Hon. Anson Herrick, M. C.

An' here's Edward Cooper,
A red-bearded throoper,
Wid his partner Hewitt—min of iron both,
An' here's Charles O'Conor,
That grim sowl of honor,
Who to thry his hand in a little free fight divarsion was niver in the laste bit lothe.

V.

Och, here's Watherberry,
Who's sore-headed—very,
Thryin' hard to bolsther up Governor Saymour's shpine;
An' there's Harry Hilton,
Who just now was kilt on
That political Jug-ornate—the Broadway line!
Here's the bould Smith Ely
For whose grieviance feel I—
Mat* thrated him badly, and there's no mistake;
An' here's Cornell (Charley),
Arm in arm wid Farley;
They are two party pilliars whom the little hayro of the Twintieth will find it hard to shake!

VI.

Here is Aldherman Froment,
Who a sturdy blow lent
To "min who take offices they don't dare to fill;"
An' the gay Dan Delavan,
Who don't fear to tell a man
What he thinks of the "grist" made in the Sixth Ward "mill;"

* M. T. Brennan, Comptroller, N. Y. City.

Here's the bully Boole, too,
Won't be made a fool, too,
So he tells the managirs they may go to—Cork;
While the gay Bill Tweedie
Owns that things looks seedy,
An' not only seedy, but most particularly dusty for the reg'lar machine candydates in our gay New York!

VII.

Och, Jim Kerrigan's howling
For the scalp of Dowling,
An' I guess he'll get it wid Billy Walsh's aid;
While grim Fifth ward Savage
Shwears to slay and ravage
If his frind Bob McIntyre ain't a Police Justice made.
Here is Billy Miner—
There's no metal finer
Than there is in Billy for a stand up fight;
An' young Aldherman Hardy,
Who is never tardy
To uphold aginst all comers—no matther how fortyfied in "conthrol" they may think themselves—the people's right.

VII.

Och, here's John McCool, too,
Who sthrikes hands wid Boole, too,
Aginst dictation, come from whence it may;
While the staunch Gid. Tucker,
Yet may bring us succor
Whin he gets his sharp pen into its full play;

Och, our great Conthroller
Needs a new consoler—
Johnny Andherson's "solace" cannot charm New York;
The machines is busted,
An' all them that thrusted
In the reg'lar nominashins (to quote the very powerful an' iligant words of my cousin Jim's boss, City Inspecther Boole), they may go to Cork!

This song, which Private O'Reilly gave with great unction on board the steam pleasure yacht which Uncle Sam is generous enough to keep for the benefit of Mr. Surveyor Andrews, appeared to create so much hilarity and was so well received, that, on its being encored, he said, with the leave of the honorable company, he'd much prefer, instead of repeating himself, to give them a song about state politics, which had been composed by his cousin, Mr. Patrick D. O'Reilly, of the 19th Ward,—" a man that needn't turn his back upon any politicianer that ever was born for downright cuteness and knowledgability." He had heard said that this song was written by Judge Waterbury, but there wasn't a word of truth in the rumor. In the first place, it wasn't the judge's sentiments. In the second, the judge had never been partial to the " Little Giant" while he was alive;

nor now was he over and above partial to General Dix, though not so "coppery" by any means as some people thought him. The last reason why the song was not Judge Waterbury's was, that it happened to be Patsy O'Reilly's; and if anybody thought it wasn't Patsy's, and would only say it wasn't Patsy's to Patsy's face any fine night, he (Private Miles) "would be happy to see the argyment," which he prophesied would be a knock down one. Patsy, his cousin, they must know had been bred for a priest, but didn't take kindly, God pity him! to the notion of single blessedness and fasting. He was too robustious a man for the church; but he had made his mark in city politics, and had to-day more contracts with the Street Department than any other one man in the city. Having got off these remarks, Private O'Reilly than sang to the air of *Bonnie Dundee*, the following verses:

SONG OF THE NATIONAL DEMOCRACY.

To the Albany chiefs the War Democrats spoke,
Ere you play the old game, there are slates to be broke;
Your words are all right, if they only were true,
But beneath the war flag you've a copperhead crew.
So fill up the cup, be it lager or bier,
Resurrect the war hatchet and sharpen the spear,
In November we'll have an almighty big row,
And to Copperhead doctrines be — well, if we bow!

Dean Richmond his stomach may pat and may pinch
His jolly red nose till it lengthens an inch;
But he can't make us think his professions are true
While he sails his war ship with a Copperhead crew.
So fill up the cup, whiskey, claret, or bier,
Resurrect the war hatchet and sharpen the spear,
There are braves on the war path prepared for a row,
And to Breckenridge doctrines be — well, if we bow!

The bold Pete de Cagger, with mystery big,
May adjust each stray hair in his amber-hued wig,
But his arts, though potential, are well understood,
If his platform be honest, why runs he with Wood?
So fill up the cup, things look certainly queer,
Resurrect the war hatchet and sharpen the spear,
With the lords of the "Central"* we're in for a row,
And to Richmond and Cagger be — well, if we bow!

* N. Y. Central Railroad.

To the tenets of Douglas we tenderly cling,
Warm hearts to the cause of our country we bring,
To the flag we are pledged—all its foes we abhor;
And we ain't for the nigger, but are for the war!
So fill up the cup, pleasant tipple is bier,
Resurrect the war hatchet and sharpen the spear;
With the Albany chiefs we are in for a row,
And their sceptre we'll break or their heads they shall bow.

It may suit the subservient Old War Horse* to say,
He is "willing to follow where Pete leads the way;"
That, with gaiety, he as blank paper will yield
Himself to the power which the Regency wield;—
Oh, so great doth your gaiety, Purdy, appear,
That we drink your good health in a bumper of bier;
And after November's slate smashing grand row,
We'll, with gaiety, make you our very best bow.

Such things do for some folks, but don't do for us,
Who for Pruyn, Cagger, Cassidy, don't care a cuss;
To the flag we are pledged, all its foes we abhor;
And first, last, all the time, we are in for the war!
So fill up the cup—healthy drinking is bier,
Resurrect the great war-axe and sharpen the spear;
In the Wigwam, next April, all factions we'll hush,
And for new men to lead, we'll go in with a rush!

The platform of Logan, Grant, Gillmore, and Dix,
Is better than any that managers fix:
—"Our flag in its glory! our Union restored,
And till treason cries Quarter, no sheath to the sword!"

* Supervisor Elijah F. Purdy.

So fill up the cup with much better than bier,
The Big Spring is bubbling, its waters are clear,
Democracy's fountain, and thus at its brink
"To the memory of Douglas" with bowed heads we drink!

We learn that Private O Reilly has been waited upon by numerous delegations from the various Irish benevolent and patriotic societies, anxious to know upon what day it will be convenient to him to receive a public demonstration of their kindliness and sympathy. To this he has very modestly replied, placing the whole matter in the hands of a committee, consisting of Judge Michael Connoly, Thomas Whelan, Esq., Mr. Andrew Carrigan, of the Emigrants' Industrial Savings Bank, Captain Patrick M. Haverty, late Quartermaster of the Irish Brigade, Mr. R. J. Lalor, and Patrick Meehan, Esq., of the *Irish American* newspaper. We learn also that arrangements are now being made for an immense and magnificent complimentary dinner to be given to Private Miles at an early day—Messrs. Charles O'Conor, James T. Brady, Richard O'Gorman, John KcKeon, Hon. Gideon Welles, Generals Sickles and Meagher, Admiral Du Pont, Peter Cooper, A. T. Stewart, Capt. C. R. P. Rodgers, A. V. Stout, Daniel Devlin, J. J. Bradley, Wm. C. Barrett, Governor Seymour, Hon.

Ben. Wood, President Lincoln, Hon. John Clancy, Daniel E. Delavan, Phineas T. Barnum, Hon. Edwin M. Stanton, Captain Fox, Captain Ericsson, Oliver Charlick, John Y. Savage, Hon. Thomas A. Ledwith, Alderman Billy Walsh, Mr. Thurlow Weed, and others too numerous to mention, being among the invited guests. We have given public dinners to all sorts of military heroes, except those of the humbler order. It now only remains for us to show, as can be done in O'Reilly's case, that even the humblest bearer of the musket is not allowed to "bloom unseen," by the keen eyes of a generous and enlightened public. Tickets for the entertainment can be had of Mr. Nathaniel Jarvis, Jr., City Hall, Judge Bartholomew O'Connor, Ann street, and Mr. A.V. Stout, at the "Shoe and Leather Bank." Dodworth's band will be in attendance, and the dinner is to be the *ne plus ultra* of Delmonico's very highest style of art. It takes place next Thursday evening; and, as there will be seats for but three hundred guests, and as the English, Russian and French Admirals, with their chiefs of staff, have been invited, all who desire to be present at this "feast of reason and flow of soul" should not lose a moment in making application for their tickets.

CHAPTER VI.

THE MILES O'REILLY BANQUET.

[From the N. Y. *Herald*, Oct. 23, 1863.

IN contrast with the magnificent banquet given to Private Miles O'Reilly, Forty-seventh regiment New York Volunteers, last evening, at Delmonico's, all previous festive entertainments of a public character given in our city must pale their ineffectual fires. The arrangements were of the most faultless kind, and the company embraced many of the very foremost representative men of Manhattan Island. The Japanese ball will hereafter be remembered as a poor affair; the Prince of Wales break-down at the Academy of Music will pass into oblivion; and even the recent civic dinner to the Muscovite Admiral and his officers, at the Astor House, will be dismissed with a contemptuous shrug when contrasted with the superb and gorgeous banquet given at Delmonico's, over which the most cultivated taste presided, and at which the ablest and most brilliant minds of the day poured out their views and aspirations with a frankness never before equalled.

THE BANQUET HALL AND BANQUET.

Delmonico, as was said of the famous bayonet charge which General Hancock did not make at Williamsburg—Delmonico "outdid himself." The tables, sparkling with massive gold and glittering silver, bore aloft, in vases of crystal and in the hands of sculptured nymphs and graces, all the most luscious fruits of the tropic and temperate zones, all the flowers of richest hue and odor. Everything that taste and liberality combined could achieve towards making the banquet worthy of those who gave it was accomplished. The dining hall was of itself a picture, so well had the artistic effects of colors in glasses, gold and silver ware, dazzling exotics, quivering jelly palaces, and crusted battlements of charlotte russe—been studied. Where the walls were not flashing mirrors, they were covered with banners of every nationality and hue—great interest being excited by the shot and shell torn banner of the Sixty-ninth New York Volunteers, which Colonel Robert Nugent, who was present, kindly volunteered for the occasion. In the window recesses were placed fanciful bowers of evergreens, liberally sprinkled with flowers, and made cool by little sparkling fountains, which sprang out of crystal basins, in which innumerable gold and silver fish were "playing at backgammon." The ornamental confectionery showed many beautiful designs, those most prominent being an exact model of Fort Sumter as it appeared before making the acquaintance of General Gillmore's rifled guns; and an Irish harper, with an Irish wolfhound at his feet and an Irish harp in his hand—for the archæological correctness of which Judge Charles P. Daly offered to give his erudite and incontrovertible certificate. The bill of fare we omit in deference to the feelings of those who were not present. Suffice it to say that Delmonico "saw" the recent Astor House Russian programme, and "went fifty better." The delicious juices of meats, the delicate flavors of fishes, the wild sweetness of game, the ravishing tenderness of fruits, the quivering sensibilities of jelly, and the sharp titillations of ice, were all present on the board in prodigal profusion and perfection.

THE CARD OF INVITATION.

The invitations issued by the committee were worded as follows:—

"SIR:—We take pleasure in inviting you to be present as a guest, on the occasion of a banquet for which we have found an excellent excuse in the person of Private Miles O'Reilly, Forty-seventh regiment New York Volunteers, late a prisoner on Morris Island, South Carolina, but released from durance vile by order of our benevolent and truly amiable President. All guests must bring with them an unlimited supply of good appetite and humor. The napkins, wines and things will be provided by our accomplished caterer.

DANIEL P. INGRAHAM,
Judge of Supreme Court.
ANTHONY L. ROBERTSON,
Judge of Superior Court.
JOHN R. BRADY,
HENRY HILTON,
Judges of Court of Common Pleas.

And seventy others, COMMITTEE OF ARRANGEMENTS for the Miles O'Reilly Banquet."

THE DISTINGUISHED GUESTS.

At half-past six precisely the guests assembled, the army being represented by Generals Truman Seymour, U.S.A.; Thomas F. Meagher, of the Irish Brigade; Alfred H. Terry, of the Tenth army corps; Lieutenant-Colonel E. W. Smith, of the Department of the South; Col. D. T. Van Buren, Captains S. W. Stockton, Horace Porter, and F. E. Howe; Lieutenant-Colonel J. H. Wilson and others; the navy by certain very distinguished officers, whose names, for reasons connected with the Navy Department, are specially omitted; the bench by Judges Bosworth,

Hilton and McCarthy; the bar by James T. Brady, Samuel J. Tilden, John Van Buren, Surrogate Tucker, Wm. M. Evarts, Daniel Lord, James W. Gerard, Richard O'Gorman, C. Bainbridge Smith, ex-Judge O'Connor, Malcolm Campbell, and many other brilliant lights, too numerous to mention; the press by Messrs. Greeley, Raymond, Hudson, Godwin, Gay, Nordhoff, Swinton, Clapp, Willis, Guernsey, and others; our business men by A. T. Stewart, Edward Cooper, Oliver Charlick, A. V. Stout, Wm. F. Havemeyer, E. H. Miller, Royal Phelps and company; the Church by the Rev. Dr. Bellows, and Chaplain Hudson, of the New York Volunteer Engineers; Congress by Messrs. Benjamin Wood, Winthrop Chanler, Anson Herrick, and Mr. Brooks of the *Express;* the heads of the city departments by Messrs. Cornell, Boole, and Devlin; the Board of Supervisors by Messrs. Ely, Purdy, Tweed, and Blunt; the Board of Aldermen by Messrs. Farley, Hardy, Chipp, Long, and Walsh; and the public generally by Professor E. Meriam, of Brooklyn Heights; David Dudley Field, Judge Edmonds, Mr. Wm. Jewett, of Colorado, and several hundred others. It was remarked, however, at this time that, owing to an oversight by the Committee of Arrangements, no sub-committee had been appointed to escort Private O'Reilly to the banquet—an oversight which was at once remedied and the Sub-committee appointed.

The following letters were received by the Committee of Arrangements and Invitations :—

TELEGRAM FROM THE PRESIDENT.

WASHINGTON, October 21, 1863.

Have to remain here watching my Cabinet. There might be a row in the family if I went away. Telegraphing not a good medium for stories; but have an anecdote appropriate to O'Reilly's case, which I send in letter by this day's mail.

LETTER FROM A DISTINGUISHED NAVAL OFFICER.

[Name omitted for reasons stated elsewhere.]

WASHINGTON, October 21, 1863.

GENTLEMEN,—I regret that a sentiment and surroundings which you can appreciate will not allow me to join your festive assembly. The Navy is not forgetful of the tribute paid by Private O'Reilly to the merit of many of its most deserving officers. In the manly pathos of his reference to the late Fleet Captain George W. Rodgers, in that song for which he suffered imprisonment, he struck strings of the human heart which must vibrate so long as courage can enkindle respect, or the death of a hero and martyr claim the tribute of a tear.

Admiral Dahlgren has had little sea experience, but no braver man lives. Few of firmer purpose or more resolute to succeed. His place, however, was in the Navy Ordnance Yard at Washington, into the habits of which he had grown; and his failure is only another exemplification of the evils which follow placing the right man in the wrong place. Thus much in justice to an old friend and valued brother officer. I think that Private O'Reilly, nevertheless, has given us honest and manly songs—songs of the kind we much need; and in the acknowledgment you propose making to him you have my earnest sympathy. With sincere respect

TELEGRAM FROM GENERAL GRANT.

CHATTANOOGA, October 21, 1863.

Your invitation reaches me just as I am preparing to move upon the enemy's works. Be assured my sympathies are with every movement which aims to acknowledge our indebtedness, as individuals and as a nation, to the private soldiers—the countless, nameless, unrewarded, often disregarded heroes of the musket and bayonet—to whose true patriotism, patient endurance, and courage in the day of danger we, who are generals, owe victory, and the country will yet owe its salvation.

LETTER FROM HON. FERNANDO WOOD.

FIFTH AVENUE, NEW YORK, October 22, 1863.

GENTLEMEN,—A recent chill blast from Ohio, coupled with a cold shiver recently caught in Pennsylvania,* have laid me up with an indisposition which confines me to that home in which I am both prized and appreciated. I look upon your banquet with a single eye to the public good; and am far from convinced that it may not soon be even a better investment to take stock in the national fortunes, than to embark with my friend Lamar in that blockade-running enterprise about which some of my foolish enemies have lately been making a fuss. Just now I am so doubled up with rheumatic twinges that my walk is slantendicular; and I make it my rule never to appear in public when in this attitude. Very candidly and sincerely yours,

* The Ohio and Pennsylvania elections.

NOTE FROM MR. WEED.

ASTOR HOUSE, 6 o'clock P.M., Oct. 22, 1863.

DEAR DEVELIN—Am just polishing off and finishing up Mayor Opdyke. Will be with you in a moment when I get through.

T. W.

LETTER FROM THE COUNT GUROWSKI.

WASHINGTON, Oct. 21, 1863.

GENTLEMEN—Your invitation is received, but me it does not suit to be of your guests invited. I, who have bearded a Russian Emperor, am not to bow in homage abject to any of the great asses who are in this country heroes made. The President (I have proved it) is a mountebank; Secretary Seward is a *faineant* and traitor; General McClellan is a traitor and ass. Chase is an ass. I have no doubt Gillmore is an assish asinine ass; as indeed are all the men whose names we in the newspapers see, or in men's mouths hear, there being only one exception, who is with highest consideration, yours,

A. GUROWSKI.

THE SECRETARY'S VISION.—Page 83.

TELEGRAPH FROM GOVERNOR SEYMOUR.

ALBANY, Oct. 22, 1863.

AM worried to death about the New York Police Commissioners. Sometimes think I will remove them; sometimes think that I won't. If I can make up my mind either one way or other, will be with you. If not, will stay here, and do nothing else but try.

FROM MR. GIDEON WELLES.

NAVY DEPARTMENT, WASHINGTON, Oct. 19, 1863.

GENTLEMEN—I regret that the severe studies and labors in which I am now engaged will not permit me to be present at your very interesting demonstration. Having commenced my investigations of naval science by a close analysis of that most famous vessel of antiquity in which the second great progenitor of our race avoided destruction—and of which, let me add, the so-called models placed in the hands of our children are even ludicrously erroneous when examined by the light of antiquarian science—I have now reached, in my descending studies, the type of vessels used in the great Spanish armada; and it is my hope, ere the termination of an existence already bountifully protracted, to have brought down my researches to that amazing new starting point in naval history—the discoveries and successful experiments of the immortal Fulton! With the introduction of steam as a motor of vessels, a great change, all will admit, has been effected in the conditions of maritime warfare. That change it is my hope, and shall be my unceasing endeavor to grasp and appreciate, if not while in official existence, then in that bright and tranquil period of repose which a grateful country will not fail to afford to the declining years of a conscientious and faithful old public servant.

Very respectfully, gentlemen.

LETTER FROM GENERAL SANDFORD.

New York, Oct. 22, 1863.

Gentlemen—As you have had the good taste to invite the members of my staff and the most prominent officers of my command, as well as myself, I thank you in their name and in my own. The managers of the late Russian banquet did differently; but those managers were members of the Common Council, which explains, if it does not palliate their offence. Their neglect in this respect extended to the Governor of the State, only one member of whose military family was asked; and to General Dix, who was invited to appear, so far as I can learn, altogether unattended, to meet foreign officers, some of equal, many of inferior, rank—but all attended by their proper retinue. I thank you again in behalf of my staff and the senior officers of the First Division, as also for myself; and beg to assure you that such of us as feel like it, will, with pleasure, avail ourselves of your very kind and hospitable invitation.

Respectfully and obediently, your servant.

Tickets were issued for only three hundred persons, but it was reported that over six hundred had squeezed themselves into the room. Mr. A. V. Stout presided admirably, and grace was said by Dr. Bellows.

After the cloth was removed, Mr. Stout introduced the intellectual part of the proceedings with some remarks, as follows:—

PRESIDENT A. V. STOUT'S SPEECH.

He said that while awaiting the return of the Subcommittee with the Guest of the Evening, he would remark that he had once before been selected to preside at a somewhat similar meeting. It was when a stand of colors was presented to the old Sixty-ninth State Militia, and a sword of honor to its Colonel, as a testimonial of our sympathy with a sentiment which made him refuse to parade an Irish regiment in honor of the Prince of Wales. (Cheers.) He was selected to preside on that occasion, probably, from the same motive which had led to his selection in the present case. It was an Irish demonstration for an Irish object and to illustrate an Irish sentiment. They therefore took an American to preside on that occasion as a token of the sympathy that exists between the American and Irish people. (Loud cheers.) That ceremony took place in peaceful times, months —though not many—before the war blast startled the North from its false dream of security. Since then the festal flag which he had an humble share in presenting had cast its flashing radiance over many a battle-field, had been lost in desperate charges of the enemy, and regained by such sacrifices of life and limb as could only fitly be described by his friend, General Thomas Francis Meagher, whose words are not less trenchant than his sword, whose genius to describe can only be surpassed by the heroism of action which has become a part of our

THE BANQUET.—Page 87.

proudest history. (Loud and long continued cheering.) To this pleasant side of his recollections of that last Irish festivity, however, there was a side which was unpleasant enough at the time, though it might appear ludicrous when mentioned now. On the very day after that demonstration, the English depositors at his bank bustled up to the counter, in one long continued current, and withdrew every dollar of theirs that was in his keeping, to the amount of many hundred thousand dollars. (Uproarious laughter, and cries of "Good, good.") He could assure them it was no laughing matter at the time, either to him or his fellow directors. Mr. Stout would now apologize for having detained them, and would introduce, during the temporary absence of Private O'Reilly, who would be present in a very few moments, the first regular toast of the evening, to which Mr. James T. Brady would respond :—

The President of the United States.

MR. JAMES T. BRADY'S SPEECH.

Mr. Brady commenced by remarking that it was a peculiarity of the race from which he came, and with which all the dearest recollections of his childhood were associated, to be diffident of their own powers and to shun all occasions of publicity, whether festive or professional. They had met that night to do honor to an humble hero—to vindicate a sentiment; and, amidst glowing fruits and the melody of ringing glasses, to renew their allegiance to the banner of the old National Democratic Faith. (Loud cheers.) Of Private O'Reilly—after whom the members of the Sub-committee were now scouring the city in carriages—it was not his part just at present to speak. He was called upon to respond to the toast of "The President of the United States;" and to that duty he would confine himself. He regretted that, by another oversight of the Committee of Arrangements—almost as bad as that by which the Guest of the Evening had not been sent for in proper form—no ladies had been invited to brighten by their smiles and inspire by their beauty such forlorn bachelors as himself. Rich as were the bouquets on the board, dazzling as were the gold and silver chasings of the plate, refreshing to the eye as were the flower-gemmed bowers of evergreens with which art had so lavishly filled the background of this brilliant picture, it needed only, but it needed still, to complete his happiness, the presence of some few representatives of that gentler sex to whom we owe our highest inspirations, our noblest virtues, and all of our purest raptures. But he was not responding to the toast of Woman—that divinity whom in childhood we adore as mother, or draw to our hearts with the sweet name of sister. He was to respond to the toast of the President of the United States, Commander-in-chief of all the land and naval forces of the Union, and to that task he would steadily address himself. (Cheers.) We neėd a country—we must have a country. As well might a forest try to preserve its freshness and vitality if torn up by the roots and cast on some granite spur of the Rocky Mountains, as for a race of men—free, intelligent, self-governing, and progressive—to exist without a nationality in whose soil should be interwoven all the roots and fibres of their being. (Loud cheers.) For himself, he had no ambition to try the experiment of supporting life without that feeling of nationality which is life's most precious stimulus. He came of a race which had long centuries ago been taught by wrongs and degradation in their native land, the full value of emigration. If the worst should come to the worst—if the twenty millions of Northern white men could not vindicate their equality, man for man, with the eight millions of the South, their numbers giving them the victory over men as brave and high-spirited as themselves—then it would be time to inquire the price of passage to New Zealand or Australia, to Otaheite or to Borneo—some land where, amidst savage solitudes or herding with savage men, we might cease to be reproached with the memories of that heritage from which our crimes, our follies, and our lack of manly qualities had driven us. (Loud applause and cheers.) There are some who lay claim to patriotism and profess themselves anxious to prosecute the war for the Union with vigor, while, in the same breath, they denounce the constitutional head of the government and all his acts with a bitterness never shown when they speak of those conspiratorial miscreants who have brought all this wretchedness and mourning on our once happy land. (Cheers and hisses.) Indeed, he had not forgotten that it was by prominent representatives of this facing-both-ways type of democracy that he had been solemnly read out of the party not many months ago, for having visited Connecticut and there performed his duty as a National Democrat—one of full growth and stature in the party, when these mushrooms of to-day were still in the rank soil out of which they have since ominously cropped—by opposing the election of Colonel Thomas H. Seymour, once his valued friend, as were these mushrooms once his very obsequious good servants. [Loud applause, and cheers, amidst which a bustle took place at the door, caused by the return of a member of the Sub-committee, who reported that he had heard from his associates, and that they had found Private O'Reilly, who would be with them in a very few moments. This announcement was received with cheers.]

Mr. Brady, when the hubbub had subsided, said that he stood where stand all the clear-headed and independent men of the country—on the platform of unfaltering and unchangeable devotion to the Union. (Loud cheers.) He cared not to discuss at present such details as the emancipation proclamation, the confiscation bill, the draft and the suspension of the habeas corpus in loyal States. Men might differ in judgment on these matters and still be the truest of true patriots. There were many measures of the administration which, in the words of General Dix, "he certainly should not have advised;" and two or three of the measures referred to might have had, if it were the time, his disapproval. But all minor issues faded out of view when we raised our eyes to the grand banner of our country, and saw its stars appealing to us for that protection in this hour of trial which heretofore they had shed upon us in every land and under all vicissitudes of fortune. (Loud and ringing cheers.) It was no idle boast ten years ago when President Franklin Pierce—(hisses, mingled with cheers and applause)—from the white steps of the Capitol spoke of that flag as "the inviolable panoply of the American citizen," no matter in what remote corner of the earth his Yankee love of adventure might have led him. (Laughter and loud cheers.) Those days would come back to us. They must. It is the vow of all the manhood of our people. In the homely words of a poet whose name, if he ever had any, had escaped the speaker's memory:—

> "To the flag we are pledged, all its foes we abhor,
> And we ain't for the nigger, but are for the war."

(Loud cheering, and cries of "Good," "That's the talk," "So say we all of us," &c.)

Our duties, if he had read their order rightly, were first to our God, next to our common country, whether ours by birth or adoption. The first of these duties he would not speak of in public. It was for the solitude of the closet, the attitude of the bent knee, and the eloquence of silent invocation. But to do our duty to our country, in its grandest and widest significance, we must, as with charity, begin at home. We must interest ourselves, however distasteful the task, in regenerating the dismal swamp of local politics. We must drain the fetid marsh now swarming with unclean things, refence the ancient boundaries of popular rights, and perform for the toads, reptiles, and other vermin which coil and swelter in those hot-beds of corruption — our local party organizations — another miracle of like character with that for which St. Patrick claims the gratitude of Ireland. (Loud laughter and cheers, continued for several minutes.) We must, he said, break up and destroy that coalition between Republicans of easy virtue and Democrats of no virtue at all, which has been the primary cause of the present degradation of politics—a degradation so utter, that to be now called a politician is almost equivalent to being called a rogue. (Cheers and laughter.) We must, above all things, and as the first step in a right direction, teach these vampires one lesson of respect for the independence of the Judiciary. From the table at which Justice sits down to measure out the priceless treasures of her uncorrupted store, their Harpy hands must be remote. They must be driven so far from the Bench, that not even in imagination can they clutch the sacred ermine, or whisper one word of entreaty, still less a threat, into the ear of those ministers upon whose purity and independence the whole fabric of a free government has its broadest and securest base. (Vociferous cheers, and loud cries of "Hilton," "Bosworth," "McCarthy," "No meddling with the Judges," &c.) Mr. Brady spoke more in sorrow than in anger—from an impulse of imperative duty. All other evils could be endured, if not cured; but let the ermine once pass under the dominion of politicians, and all assurances of personal freedom and property would be at the mercy of the basest and most unscrupulous class of the community. He spoke, it might be said, with feeling—with interest—and he was not ashamed to own it. He did feel outraged by the attempt now being made against the official life of his friend, the upright man, the honest jurist, Henry Hilton. (Cheers.) His friend, the upright man, the honest jurist, Mr. Bosworth. (Renewed cheering.) His friend, the upright, kindly, and whole-souled Judge Florence McCarthy. (Vociferous shouts of "They shan't do it," "They can't," &c.) Of one of the candidates put up against one of the gentlemen he had named, he felt it but justice to speak in terms of personal commendation.* Under other circumstances, it would have given him pleasure to support one of the adverse nominees for the Superior Court, assured of his integrity, his talents and his capacity. (Hear, hear.) But situated as these matters now were, it had become the first duty of every good citizen to trample down all considerations of personal liking or disliking, and to lend his every effort to the task of preserving unimpaired and in all the fresh lustre of its purity the independence of those officers who are entrusted, in last resort, with the maintenance of all the rights which are dearest to us as free citizens of a great and civilized republic. (Applause.)

SOME ANXIOUS INQUIRIES.

At this point the bustle at the door was renewed, and loud cries announced the return of another member of the Sub-Committee, of whom eager inquiries were made as to the whereabouts of Private O'Reilly, the Bard of Morris Island. The Sub-Committee man explained that he had heard that Pri-

* Judge Lemuel B. Garvin.

vate O'Reilly had been overtaken some half hour before by the associate who had previously returned, and that he had come there expecting to find the Guest of the Evening in the seat of honor. The matter was annoying enough, but there could be no doubt but that the other members of the Sub-Committee would soon be back and bring the Guest of the Evening with them. This assurance satisfied the audience, more especially when it became known that one of the Sub-Committee had gone to the residence of Mr. James O'Reilly, in the Sixteenth Ward, where Private Miles was awaiting the carriage.

Order being once more restored, the Chairman said that, in the absence of the gallant soldier whom they had all met to honor, he would propose the next regular toast of the evening—" Our Army and our Navy."

SPEECH OF MR. LUKE CLARK, OF MORRIS ISLAND.

On this the hubbub was renewed with increasing clangor, various cries being raised for "Meagher," "Terry," "Sickles," "Graham," "Let us have Halleck himself," "Little Mac's the boy," &c. While the confusion was at its height, a sturdy Irishman named

Luke Clark of the 5th Ward, lifted himself on one of the chairs and demanded to know—What had the Sub-committee done with Private Miles O'Reilly? Some were beginning to say that the committee had sold him for a substitute—perhaps to go in place of Mr. Theodore Tilton, of the *Independent*, or of Mayor Oydyke's son, both of whom were drafted. He had known Miles down on Morris Island, and knew he was too decent a boy and too good a judge of a good dinner to stay away from such a feast of his own accord. He (the speaker) had thrown up as many shovels full of dirt with his own two good looking hands on Morris Island as the next man; and he appealed to General Terry and Lieutenant Colonel Smith, who were both present, to see justice done to him. (Cheers and renewed demonstrations.)

DR. CARMICHAEL'S SONG.

In order to restore harmony, Dr. Carmichael was here introduced, and sang with excellent spirit and voice the following song, composed by "a gentleman of this city," whose name, unfortunately, our reporter was not able to catch. The Doctor has a delicious voice, brilliantly cultivated; and gave the following words to the air of "When the twilight bat is flitting," with an earnestness, pathos, and tenderness which could not have been surpassed:

THE CAPTAIN'S DAUGHTER.

'Twas a bright expanse of water,
Where the Captain's gentle daughter
Every summer morning sought her
Bath of beauty, light and grace;
Quite a fleet of drifted lilies
Danced above the mimic billows,
And a screen of drooping willows
Curtained close the bathing place.

In my skiff at random floating,
Rod and line but little noting—
Ah! what subtle charm had boating
Since the bathing place was known!
"Happy waves that may enfold her!"
And my fancy growing bolder
Changed each lily to a shoulder
White and dimpled as her own!

"Ah! how clear!" I muttered, eyeing,
Many a colored pebble lying
Far below, and vainly trying
On some book to fix my thought;
"Now some good breeze, hither winging,
Set yon silver curtain swinging—
Coolness to the bather bringing!"
But the good breeze answered not.

Homeward o'er the meadows tripping,
All the lovelier for her dipping,
Soon I saw the maiden skipping,
Who said gravely when we met:
"Friend, thou hast grown fond of boating"—
And my weak heart quailed on noting
The malicious laughter floating
In the eyes of my coquette.

This song was received, as any song by Dr. Carmichael is sure to be, with vehement applause; on the subsidence of which the Chairman said that he was now about to propose, "The Health of Miles O'Reilly," on which subject, before they drank it, his friend Judge Charles P. Daly would make a few remarks, so well timed that they should only cease on the appearance of their absent guest. (Laughter and cheers.)

SPEECH OF JUDGE DALY.

Judge Daly regretted that, having been absent in the bridal party of General Michael Corcoran, he had not time to prepare as he could have wished for this occasion. All were aware that he traced his origin to that "Green Isle" in which their absent guest first knew the blessings of a mother's smile and the wholesome nourishment of potatoes (Loud laughter.) The practice of receiving, without regard to rank, those who have faithfully served their country in the field, is of remote antiquity. He had found in the course of his artistic, antiquarian and archæological researches that a similar compliment had once been paid to a non-commissioned officer in the army of Wallenstein, during the Thirty Years' War, as mentioned by the learned historian, Von Schneidermark. In the early histories and traditions of the Scandinavians also, such instances were not uncommon. Count Ptosotoff, the earliest historian of Rnssian Tartary, mentions no less than three cases of a similar character, and of all these the famous Gen. Kütsoff speaks in terms of commendation. He trusted that these citations from high authority would completely satisfy everybody ——

AN INTERRUPTION.

Mr. Clark again raised himself upon a chair, declaring that he was ready to admit, for argument sake, that the old lords and gentlemen Judge Daly had just named might be very respectable people in their way; but nothing could "completely satisfy" him—nothing that Mr. Wallenstein, or Mr. Putusoff, or Mr. Cutusoff could do or say, until the Sub-committee could be made to account for what they had done with his friend and countryman. (Loud applause, and cries of "That's the talk, Luke;" "They've sold him as a substitute.")

SPEECH OF LIEUTENANT-COLONEL E. W. SMITH.

As Mr. Clark had referred to General Terry and to himself, Colonel Smith had a few words to say. As an officer of the Department of the South he had known Private Miles O'Reilly, and had, in fact, signed the very furlough on which Private O'Reilly was now in their midst. (Loud cries and laughter. "He ain't in our midst;" "That's what's the matter," &c.) As an officer of the regular army, it was somewhat against his sense of discipline to sit at a banquet where a private soldier was present as a guest. (Here again broke out cries—"He ain't present;" "Wish he were." "It's all Putusoff and Cutusoff with the Sub-committee.") Colonel Smith would be compelled to resume his seat if these interruptions were continued. He knew Private O'Reilly, and he also had known Mr. Luke Clark while that patriot was working in the trenches. Luke, if he remembered rightly, had been in the employ of a sutler, and was condemned to spadework in the parallels for having given more whiskey to some soldiers than was good for them. (Roars of laughter, and cries of "Good boy, Luke.") As to the labors performed by the army under General Gillmore in the Department of the South, he felt that words were inadequate to describe their vastness. (Loud cheers.) No description, however, could be more perfect than that given in one stanza of the now famous song, for which Private O'Reilly had first fallen under the Provost Marshal's censure. He referred to the stanza commencing:

'Tis no harm, you seem to think,
That upon destruction's brink—
He is not the boy to shrink—
    Our gallant Gillmore stands;
Holding hard his threatened lines,
Pushing far his saps and mines.

That was just it. If ever lines were "held hard," Gillmore's had been when they first captured Morris Island. For months one half the army was up all night in the trenches, with spade and pick, while the other half stood guard against the enemy with the bayonet.

A VOICE.—What might the third half be doing? (Laughter.)

GENERAL GILLMORE FOR NEXT PRESIDENT.

Colonel Smith then paid a high tribute to the qualities of Generals Sherman and Hunter, the former commanders of the Department of which he had now the honor to be an humble officer; and before resuming his seat would only propose the health of General Q. A. Gillmore, the hero of Pulaski and Sumter; and might the country never have a worse fate than to have such a man for its next President. (Uproarious applause.)

TRIUMPHANT RETURN OF THE SUB-COMMITTEE.

Just at this moment volleys of cheers and joyful shouts from the staircase announced that the long expected Sub-committee were at length approaching. "Have yez Miles O'Reilly wid you?" shouted a burly Hibernian, elbowing his way through the crowd, and leaning over the staircase. "We have James O'Reilly, his cousin," was the answer, "and Miles, he says, is amongst you, only that he is in plain clothes, so that you don't know him."

GREAT QUESTION OF THE DAY—"ARE YOU MILES O'REILLY?"

The confusion following this announcement was perfectly indescribable. Every man turned round to his neighbor, seized his elbow, looked square into his eyes, and asked eagerly—"Are you Private Miles?" Everybody asked the question of every other person, and every person said "No" to everybody.

Mr. Luke Clark said he had been all round the tables, and couldn't see Miles anywhere. He asked that the Sub-committee should be seized, and never let go until they gave him up. (Hear, hear.) The more he thought of it the surer he felt that they had sold the Guest of the Evening for a substitute to either Tilton or Opdyke. The Sub-committee were a collection of Judases, and he was individually in favor of at once holding them personally responsible for the production of their missing friend. (Immense applause, followed by the immediate institution of threatening demonstrations against the committee.)

SPEECH OF HON. BEN WOOD.

Mr. B. Wood rose as the friend of "Peace." He was for "Peace," under all circumstances, and for submission as the means of attaining it. To say that his views, if carried out, would degrade the North, was folly, which no sensible man, who knew the worth of "Peace," could believe. All he wished on behalf of the South—with one of whose "peculiar institutions" his own fortunes were largely connected—all he wished was, that we should withdraw our armies from every square foot of soil south of Mason and Dixon's line, divide our navy into two, giving the South half, accept the Montgomery constitution, and confer on Mr. Jeff. Davis the Loyal Union League nomination for the next Presidency. [Groans, hisses and hootings. Loud cries of "Put him out," "Scotch the copperhead," and so forth. Mr. Ben Wood kept on gesticulating, and shouting—the only words we could catch being "four, eleven, forty-four or fight."]

A PRESIDENTIAL SONG.

Mr. John E. Develin at last made himself heard above the tumult. He wished to introduce to the meeting ex-Coroner Frank O'Keefe, who would now give them a song in the chorus of which all present he knew would gladly join—his friends General Terry and Colonel Smith not least. Thus introduced, Mr. O'Keefe sang the following stanzas to the well-known West Point and old army air of "Benny Havens," which is the American edition of "Irish Molly."

Come fill your glasses, fellows,
The night is wearing low;
A health to Quincy Gillmore
Let us drink before we go.
He's the victor of Pulaski,
And he it was, we know,
Who knocked Fort Sumter into a
Triangular chapeau.
So fill your glasses, fellows,
The night is wearing low;
A health to Quincy Gillmore
Let us drink before we go.

Oh, a bumper to Ulysses Grant,
A chief whose worth we know;
Our banner in his stalwart hands,
What reck we of the foe?
He's the Mississippi river horse—
Resistless as its flow,
And all its length of waters
With his victories are aglow.

So a bumper to Ulysses Grant,
A chief whose worth we know;
Our banner in his stalwart hands,
What reck we of the foe?

The applause which followed these verses was flattering not only to Mr. O'Keefe, but to the generals thus mentioned. By unanimous consent the song was encored, and the applause was, if any thing, louder, and the chorus heartier, when sung the second time.

CHIEF ENGINEER DECKER'S SPEECH.

Mr. Decker said he had been to a good many fires and had helped to put out a good many. But there was one fire he would never try to extinguish—that of patriotism. (Enthusiastic cheers.) He had run with a good many "machines;" but the shakiest machine he ever had run with was that joint-stock-consolidated engine company, called the Tammany-Mozart "Little Six." It was pretty well played out. (Loud cries of "Hi, hi!" and groans for the Tammany-Mozart managers.)

SPEECH OF MR. OLIVER CHARLICK.

Mr. Charlick desired to be allowed the floor, if only for one moment, in order to reply to the denationalized, the undemocratic sentiments in which Mr. Benjamin Wood had recently indulged. He could not but attribute the present false attitude of a great portion of the Democratic party in this City and State to the miserable kind of material that was now in control of the regular Democratic machine-organizations of Manhattan Island. The council fires of Tammany may be lighted, but where are the great braves and warriors who once sat there, toasting their shins in the good days gone by? Where now are such men as Charles O'Conor, George Douglas, John J. Cisco, Edwin Croswell, Churchill C. Cambreling, Samuel J. Tilden, Greene C. Bronson, Wm. F. Havemeyer, John Targee, C. W. Lawrence, De Witt Clinton, Gulian C. Verplanck, John A. Dix, Azariah Flagg, Daniel D. Tompkins, and all that glorious old galaxy who once sat in the Conventions of our party, and ruled its destinies with the solemnity and conscientiousness of the Council of Elders in the best days of the Venetian republic? Have we any successors to these men? Contrast the names recited with those which are prominent in politics to-day. Every great man in our city Israel is excluded merely because he is a great man—too great to be cramped to the pattern of spoil coalitions

—too pure to be allowed inside the charnel-house in which lie mouldering the sad remains of democratic principle. Charles O'Conor is outside the organization to-day; James T. Brady has been read out of the party by the managing leaders, and so has Gen. Dix; Henry Hilton and Florence McCarthy are to be slaughtered; Bosworth is a phœnix expiring amidst the flames of petty wrath and jealousy. (Cheers.) But, gentlemen, to birds of this description there is a certain resurrection, and from its ashes we shall yet see arising a fresh and revivified democracy. Gentlemen, I am of the opinion that "freedom's battle once begun" will require a great deal of good management to make it stop.

ANOTHER INTERRUPTION—FIERCE CRIES FOR O'REILLY.

Whatever more Mr. Charlick might have intended to say was here lost amidst the yellings, cries, stamping, and other noises, which the friends of Private Miles, and those anxious to see him, now raised. Mingled with these were the criminations and recriminations of the various members of the Sub-Committee of Arrangements, each saying that it was the duty of the other to have invited the Guest of the Evening, and to have called for him in a carriage at the proper time. Mr. James O'Reilly gave it as his opinion that his cousin Miles had never received any official invitation, it being everybody's business to invite him, and, therefore, nobody doing it. There was never one of the Reillys who wanted to thrust his company anywhere. He thought that Miles had the family pride, and had stayed away to show that, though only a private soldier, he had still in his veins the thrue O'Reilly blood.

COLORADO JEWETT'S REMARKS.

Mr. Jewett, of Colorado, here produced a large manuscript, and said that, with the permission of the company, he would now proceed to read for them an exposition of the exact state of his peace and gold negotiations with the various crowned heads of Europe, with all of whom he was on terms of personal intimacy. This announcement was followed by loud cries of "Oh, shut up," "Print it in the *Tribune*," &c., amidst which Mr. Jewett indignantly withdrew.

MR. FRANK O'DONNELL'S SONG.

In order to amuse the company while they were waiting, Mr. Frank O'Donnell kindly volunteered to give them a song, the authorship of which is ascribed to ex-Judge Bartholomew O'Connor. Mr. O'Donnell sings delightfully, and his lyric, of which we append a copy, is called—

THE SPRIG OF TAMMANIA.

AIR—*The Sprig of Shillelah.*

Oh, self is the soul of a politic man—
He loves a neat office and gets what he can,
  The young sprig of Tammania, the Tammany prig!
He goes up to Albany, eager for spoil,
Comes down, holds a caucus to "make the pot boil;"
Then believes he has got full control of the town,
And he hopes on his "gridiron" to do us all brown,
  The young sprig of Tammania, the Tammany prig!

Who had ever the luck to see Tammany Hall
When the true men who sat there were patriots all,
  Old sachems of Tammany—Tammany braves!
They spoke to a party of principle then—
To a party not ruled by unprincipled men:
They knew not of "spoil coalitions" with those
Who in public they'd make us believe to be foes,
  Those old sachems of Tammany—Tammany braves!

There's a truth, mighty leaders, we'd have you to know,
We've been waiting to see just how far you would go,
  You sprigs of Tammania, you very bad prigs!
And now, when the country is sore and distressed,

Its brave soldiers fighting, its martyrs at rest,
Be sure that the people, so quick to descry,
Will give *you*, ere you know it, a very black eye,
You bad sprigs of Tammania, you very bad prigs!

GRAND BURST UP OF THE BANQUET.

How much longer Mr. O'Donnell might have continued singing, nobody can tell, as he appeared fresh and had any number of additional verses in his head. But the excitement about the continued non-appearance of the Guest of the Evening now rose almost to the point of frenzy, and threatened to assume some violent shape. Loud objurgations were heaped on the Sub-Committee of Arrangements for their gross neglect in not inviting and properly escorting Private Miles O'Reilly to the banquet. It was in vain that Surveyor Andrews offered the use of his government steam yacht to scour the bay, go up to Albany, or cross over to Ireland, in pursuit of the absent guest. He was received with much the same cries as had greeted Mr. Colorado Jewett; but peace was partially restored when Mr. Gideon J. Tucker proposed that all present should resolve themselves into a Committee of the Whole for the purpose of hunting up the missing hero. Several more songs were sung before our reporters left, but the noise was too great for them to catch the words, the fun growing too fast and furious for weak heads. The steadier portion of the audience left by the back exit as rapidly as they could just about this time; and we deem it just as well, if not a little better, to here drop the curtain. The play of "Hamlet," with the part of the Prince left out, will not again be repeated.

CHAPTER VII.

MILES GOING INTO CITY POLITICS.

WE learn, said the *Herald*, one day,—just as the November election in New York City and State was being cleared off, and the municipal campaign for December opening,—We learn that Private Miles O'Reilly, Forty-seventh regiment New York Volunteers, is about to devote himself to a reconsolidation of all the political interests in this city, on the simple basis of the "spoils." He thinks, by throwing aside all clap-trap of principle or patriotism, and uniting all the now warring elements of the political family in an immense Joint-Stock-Consolidated-Grand-Junction-Lobby-League, that the managers on all sides will be enabled to fill their pockets much more readily and with much less trouble to themselves. His idea is to take the total assessed value of all property, real and personal, on Manhattan Island, as his "base of operations;" and to make arrangements for its absorption at the rate of twenty-five per cent. per annum by his new political company. Shares will be issued to all existing political interests, on the same strict system that was observed in providing for the stockholders of the "Consolidated Stage Company" in the city railroad legislation at Albany during the last half dozen years. We learn further that Private O'Reilly, in order to carry out these views, has issued a caucus circular calling together all the parties in interest, for the purpose of arranging the details and settling the apportionment of stock which is to be given to each. This caucus meets at the St. Nicholas to-morrow evening, and its proceedings will doubtless prove of the highest interest. The only objection of any weight that we have heard urged against Private O'Reilly's plan is, that his organization cannot be permanent, as, in four years, at twenty-five per cent. per annum, it will have absorbed all the property, real and personal, of the city, and there will be "nothing left to steal." To this Private O'Reilly answers that, when all the taxpayers have been turned out into the streets, full means of activity will still be left to the organization in plots and efforts to cheat each other. "Inside rings" will then have to be formed, having for their object a further "consolidation" of plunder. He is also sanguine that, with the triumph of the scheme in this city, politicians all over the State and country may take it up, until finally it shall be placed in a position to dictate one of its own members or agents for the next Presidency. The proceedings of the caucus will be looked for with interest.

"OUR REPORTER."

CHAPTER VIII.

THE MILES O'REILLY CAUCUS. AN INTRODUCTION AFTER THE MANNER OF THE "WORLD."

IF on the proper day of the proper month, several hundred years before the commencement of the Christian era, the chief editor of the Athens *Herald* had sent out one of his reporters of an afternoon, with orders to bring back an exact account of the Eleusinian Mysteries—to reveal any of which to the uninitiated incurred the penalty of death—the feelings of that reporter might not have been of the most festive character. We fancy him securing his stylus and tablets next to his manly breast, taking an affectionate farewell of the wife who weeps and the children who cling to him; then, wrapping around him his reportorial toga and drawing tighter the strings of his sandals, so that he may be prepared, if need be, to make the best time ever witnessed in the Olympic games. Finally we see him drop on one knee, raise his eyes to the white porch of his home, breathe a hasty invocation to the Gods of the Acropolis, then pull down his ivy wreath over his eyes, and dash off madly towards the scene of the mystic and sacred ceremonials.

HOW OUR REPORTER ENTERED THE CAUCUS ROOM.

Human nature, even in the reportorial form, is much the same now as it was three thousand years ago; and as the Athenian reporter, in toga and sandals, would have felt while endeavoring to gain admission as a "dead-head" to the Eleusinian rites, so felt your reporter, in stove-pipe hat and Wellingtons, while attempting to gain entrance to the initial caucus of the new political organization, known as the "Joint Stock Consolidated Grand Junction Lobby League," with which the name of Private Miles O'Reilly, Forty-seventh Regiment, New York Volunteers, has been recently connected. What would have been his fate if compelled to remain outside in the immense and indescribable jam of humanity which awaited the regular opening of the doors, it is not for him to say. Ribs have only a certain strength, and the crushing in of the breast-bone upon the spine is not good treatment for consumptive patients. Fortunately, however, he found a "next friend" (such things are useful and plentiful in politics), who took him round to a private entrance in rear of the caucus room, where Messrs. Dick Connolly and Sal. Skinner were on duty as janitors. These gentlemen he at once recognized by their regalia as promising knights of the "Most illustrious D. B. Order;" and on giving them the pass-word and grip of an "arch-past" he was at once allowed to enter the mystic chamber, fifteen or twenty minutes in advance of its being thrown open to the rush of the regular caucus representatives.

THE CORPUS DELICTI IN COURT—MODEL OF THE CITY OF NEW YORK.

The room selected for the caucus, in the St. Nicholas Hotel, was one of great size, oblong in form, —its rear windows very appropriately commanding a fine view of Mercer street. Towards this end there was a large stage, about three feet high, and covered with green baize, which ran across the room; and on this stage there was an exact model of the city of New York—all its streets laid out, all its church spires visible; every house, store and shanty having its counterpart in miniature, and many of its public parks and squares still showing traces of having been used as encampments. Thousands of beautiful models of sailing vessels and steamers lay moored around the piers. On this gentle slope stands Murray Hill. There is the City Hall. The Park, with all its winding roads, woody ravines, glassy lakelets, magnificent bridges, breezy hills and odorous garden patches, lies exposed to view. Here, at Fort Washington, the primeval rock pushes up one shoulder through the trimly shaven grass in rear of James Gordon Bennett's house. This is the highest point of Manhattan

THE CAUCUS.—Page 120.

Island. There are palaces all along the North river. Very splendid, too, is that portion of the city north of Fourteenth street, and west of Third avenue. That black open space on Fifth avenue is where the Colored Orphan Asylum lately stood. You see similar black spaces in Third avenue and elsewhere. These are the vestigia nigra of our late anti-draft, anti-negro riot. But of all the pretty things in the model, Broadway is the prettiest and most picturesque. Its architecture so various, its idiosyncrasies so peculiar! Here the new style is for ever jostling out or dwarfing into insignificance the old. There are banners on every roof. This, verily, is a great city, and great should be the men who rule it. This city is certainly worth subjugation and spoliation. Are there not "patriots" enough in it to successfully essay the task?

POLITICAL ASPECTS OF THE MODEL, SHOWING WHERE THE POWER LIES.

In looking at this model, so exact in all its details, an irregularity of proportion becomes apparent, and in this irregularity is its political significance. The shanties in Mackerelville are as large or larger than many fine mansions in the best avenues. Small groggeries, in this model, are two or three times the size of vast public institutions—such as school-houses or churches, in whose shade they nestle. The City Hall towers up on high, as though its cupola were in the clouds, while its base spreads out to a bulk which threatens soon to reach from river to river, and to absorb half the island. Such political buildings as Tammany Hall, Mozart Hall, the Police Headquarters, the Republican Headquarters, the "Pewter Mug," the "Ivy Green," the Comptroller's office and other municipal offices, and all the tenement houses throughout the city, are built in harmony with the proportions of the exaggerated City Hall, and out of all harmony with their actual neighbors. On looking closer it may be seen that a complete network of powerful threads and wires connects together in bonds of telegraphic sympathy and accord all buildings modelled in this larger proportion. The nearer it is examined the stronger and more complex will appear the system of wire-work which radiates from the City Hall in all directions. There are wires, powerful and numerous, and each dripping with corrupt gold, leading to the site of every contract famous in municipal history. There are wires to the Battery enlargement;

wires to every one of the city railroads now being built; wires to every ferry franchise; wires to every pier and dock; wires to the Russian and all other banquets; hundreds of wires to Washington market, and hundreds upon hundreds yet quivering with electric life and connecting the Fort Gansevoort market-site with the sources of authority. From every street and engine-house, from every road and avenue, from every grant and privilege, from every police precinct and from certain of the courts and other offices, a network of tributary wires runs back to the City Hall, and is from thence re-distributed to the Tammany, Mozart, and Republican Head-quarters. A cable, very fine in itself, but made of four thicker and seventeen thinner strands, connects this whole complex mechanism with the State Capitol at Albany—an exact and striking model of which was placed upon a pedestal some few feet behind the model of the City, just as the Capitol itself looks down from its lofty eminence when viewed from the foot of State street. This cable thus forms, as it were, the rein or guiding strap with which the master charioteers at Albany disport themselves while driving the "city team." The clock in the cupola of the City Hall, we should add, had a musical box attached to its machinery, which, as time slipped on, poured forth such popular airs as "That's the way the money goes," and "Come, brothers, join the mystic ring," in one continuous melody.

ONE OF THE MODEL-MAKERS ADMIRES HIS OWN WORK.

While your reporter was examining this model, a deep, gruff voice said, just close to him; "Curious, isn't it?" and turning sharply round he found himself face to face with a great burly figure of the live oak type, clad in solemn black. He was an elderly man, of rough and shaggy appearance, with masses of bushy grey hair, heavy and shaggy grey eyebrows; dark, piercing grey eyes, a heavy and curling beard running around his lower jaw; brown complexion, a short, thick, aggressive nose, and cheeks rather inclined to look dropsical. In the lines of his strong, coarse mouth there lurked infinite force and cunning, and his face, as a whole, could be extremely expressive, or as stolid and meaningless as though cut in timber. "Very curious, isn't it?" he repeated, with that tender interest which a workman of high order feels in examining some masterpiece of ingenuity which has had his own best efforts. "I quite pride myself on that model," he added.

"Three-fourths of its present machinery I invented and put up with my own hands."

GRAND ENTRANCE OF THE DELEGATIONS—BLUE LIGHTS BURNING.

Just at this moment the main doors leading into the hall were thrown open, and in poured such a tide of humanity as is seldom witnessed in one assemblage. First came a select delegation from Tammany Hall, headed by several illustrious corporators in the Broadway and other city railroads, while its rear was brought up by Messrs. Peter Griese, Martin J. Kopp, J. Joseph Donelly, John H. Doty, E. S. Williams, and other well known public characters of that order. Next came a select Mozart delegation—very select, indeed—consisting of the Duke of Bloomingdale, the whole Tobacco Family, three judicial candidates, seventeen candidates for the Assembly, four candidates for the Senate, eight candidates for Aldermen and twenty-four candidates for the Board of Councilmen. After these came the Republican delegation, led by the burly and graceful forms of the West Washington market, Fort Gansevoort, Ferry franchise and Marine transportation Operators, the rear being brought up and kept in order by the batons of three prominent gentlemen from Police Headquarters. These were the only bodies that entered the caucus room with any show of organization; but behind them poured in any imaginable quantity of "roughs" and expectants, fellows with gun contracts and fellows without; Belgian and Russ pavement contractors, jobbers and lobbyists, and numerous representatives of that semi-legal class who only use the bar as an excuse for corruption. There were emigrant runners, policy-shop keepers and their backers, baggage smashers, pocket-book droppers, and all the other classes powerful in politics; while mixed up with all these were some few dozen of our very best citizens, who evidently came there prompted by a public-spirited curiosity to have one good look at the kind of rulers under whose control this fair City has passed. Just as this assemblage was pouring in, several large blue lights which had been placed all round the model of the devoted city were set on fire, and as they illuminated the faces of the entering crowd with their ghastly glare, the effect was equal to any thing in the best "bandit pictures" of Salvator Rosa.

LAW AND ORDER VICTORIOUS—THE CHAIR IS FILLED.

While everything was still in confusion, the leading men of the three regular delegations made obeisance to the rough and shaggy old man who claimed to have made three-fourths of the model. They hailed him as "King of the Lobby," and moved that, as a matter of right and to protect his own and their interests, he should take the chair. They assured him they had "all the sinew" necessary to put through a "Fifth of August," or any other scheme they saw fit. To this the shaggy man grunted a hoarse assent, shuffled into a large arm chair, which was placed just between the models of the Albany State House and the city of New York, then seized his mallet and commenced rapping vigorously while calling "Order, order," in stentorian tones. To this the assemblage, now pretty well seated, replied by cries of "Law and order forever," "We have Law and the profits on our side," etc.

SPEECH OF THE CHAIRMAN—THE PROGRAMME STATED.

The Chairman was a man of business—a strictly commercial man—and would go to business at once. He announced that the first caucus of the "Miles

O'Reilly Joint Stock Consolidated Grand Junction Lobby League" was now in session, its object being to form a political company which, "taking as its base of operations all property, real and personal, on Manhattan Island, should make arrangements for its absorption at the rate of twenty-five per cent. per annum amongst the members of said Lobby League." There were other clauses providing for the formation of "inside rings," to cheat each other, whenever the main design against all present property-holders should have been thoroughly carried out. (Loud applause.) The Chairman had now to call their attention to a grave matter. All knew that Governor Seymour had vetoed a bill last winter. (Painful groans.) For that offence against the interests of certain leaders he should never be forgiven. (Loud cheers.) The day of vengeance was almost within their grasp; and he had now to denounce Horatio Seymour as a traitor to the principles and candidates of the democratic party. (Loud applause.) He had documents to prove that Governor Seymour had subscribed no less than sixteen thousand dollars to the funds of the Republican party this very year. (Loud cheers.) The Governor had retained in power the Police Commissioners, and they had just levied an assessment of sixteen thousand dollars upon the men and officers of their force, with which to defeat the democratic party. (Here there were some symptoms of a row.) The Chairman cared little, personally, which party succeeded. He had belonged to all parties—and had made money out of all. But as they owed Governor Seymour a grudge, bitter and lasting, for his veto of the Broadway Railroad Bill, he thought all the Governor's "friends" should circulate this story as widely as they could. (Applause, and cries of "We will, we will," etc.)

SPEECH OF HIS SERENE HIGHNESS THE DUKE OF BLOOMINGDALE.

The Duke of Bloomingdale here rose, and in his most Henry Clayish manner, pulled forward the peaks of his shirt-collar, then stuck his right hand into the breast of his buttoned surtout, and, extending his left hand oratorically, thus commenced:—He announced to the assembled wisdom that he and his associates, Mr. Peter Griese of Tammany, one of the grantees of the Broadway Railroad, and the Republican representative from West Washington market, had held an election in their own minds, taken the votes of all present on all the questions that would arise during the evening, and were prepared, in conjunction with their worthy Chairman, to carry out all the details of the meeting on the basis of popular representation thus secured. (Loud cries of "Hi, hi," "Bully for you," etc.) He would advert for a moment to the declaration of their worthy Chairman that this was a business meeting, and should be conducted on strictly commercial principles. ("Hear, hear.") The preponderance of stock in the "Joint Stock Consolidated Grand Junction Lobby League" had already passed into the hands of the Chairman, the two friends he had just named—representing the Tammany and Republican "machines"—and into his own, representing the Mozart interest. (Dead silence and blank faces among the audience.) He must ask his "friends,", as Governor Seymour would say, to have confidence in him. Confidence was one of the softest, tenderest, and most useful sentiments of the human heart. ("Hear, hear.") Without confidence between man and wife there would be jealousy and wretchedness. Without confidence between partners there would be all kinds of trouble. ("Hear, hear," and laughter.) Without confidence, said *Punch*, there could be no enjoyment of sausages. He needed confidence, and asked all his friends to place their interests in his hands. Indeed, by the arrangements already perfected, they were so placed already, and any who did not like it could do otherwise. (Blanker and blanker faces amongst the crowd.) He would say, however, on commercial principles, that some nominations for December were yet in his hands. ("Hear, hear.") And about these he would be happy to see any gentlemen who were aspirants at his private office. (Faces growing blank again.) He would now introduce to them his friend, Mr. Peter Griese, who would explain to their satisfaction so much of the scheme of the new "Joint Stock Consolidated Grand Junction Lobby League" as he might think it fit for them to know. (Loud cheers.)

SPEECH OF THE HON. PETER GRIESE, BROADWAY CORPORATOR.

Mr. Griese was of opinion that men have their affinities as well as metals. He had once been separated from his friend, the last speaker. That friend once had power, and he had none. There was, therefore, between them no basis for a fair and equitable division of interests. Finally the speaker obtained some power, no matter how. ("Hear,

hear.") A division of interests was then agreed upon, and the moment this was accomplished, they rushed into each other's arms like long-lost brothers. (Loud applause.) They felt that they were truly congenial souls. (Deep sensation, during which the noble Duke used his pocket-handkerchief quite freely, either to wipe his eyes or hide his laughter.) Mr. Griese said that all had heard of the "Tammany machine," the "Mozart machine," and the "Republican machine." But they had now before them, in that beautiful model of their city—all its political interests bound together by the ligatures of a common interest, and all its "placers" and "pockets" so brilliantly and appropriately illumined by the mellow radiance of a blue light—in this model, he said, they had the true secret, the cabalistic mystery, the philosopher's stone, so to speak, of all the "machines" put together! This was the magic machine which turned everything that it touched into gold. This it was which had power to seize even the judiciary by the throat and squeeze gold out of its decisions. Nothing was good but gold; power was the key to gold, and had no other value. The model before them was one to which he had contributed many wires, and the full worth of its every wire he knew. With the kind aid of the Police Commissioners, the present leaders, he thought, could hold their grip. (Loud applause.) All knew how far it was from his nature to seek personal aggrandizement in politics. ("Hear, hear.") All knew, or should know—and he was prepared to expel any man who did not—the thoroughly unselfish and generous structure of his heart. (Loud cheers.) But while he could not, would not, and never did, wish anything for himself, he had "friends," in whose behalf he was ready to demand that everybody else should make every sacrifice. Men, he continued, like those friends of his youth whose names, like his own, were inserted in the Broadway Railroad Bill. Men, it is true, unknown to fame, unknown even to the Directory; but none the less near and dear to him. Men who might be "myths," and mere swindling ghosts or *simulacra* of Corporators to those vagabond Hessians of the press who were arrayed against all the little generosities of legislation by which millions of the public treasure were annually given away; but who were precious to him as the apple of his own eye, and for whom he was ready, he again repeated, to demand that everything else should be sacrificed. (Loud applause.) He wished them all to know that the opposition to their schemes amounted to nothing. The insurrectionary, national, or loyal men of the city Democracy had no organization, no "machine" that was worth anything. For the people he cared nothing. In his lexicon, "the masses" were always written "them asses." (Laughter and applause.) As to the pretence made that certain Democrats were opposed to corruption, to lobby intrigues, to shares in fraudulent contracts, and so forth, this was all "poppycock." He judged men by himself. That was the only standard of measure they had to go by; and he knew, after much self-study, that no men living were actuated by pure, patriotic, or disinterested motives. These terms were words, mere words and nothing more. He himself had once joined in raising the cry: "Honest men against cheats." By this he had convinced the cheats that it would be cheaper to "let him in" than to keep him out—and that was all he wanted. His own experience told him that there were no honest men in public life—no honest motives. These things he knew, and would believe nothing to the contrary. (Loud applause.)

AN INTERRUPTION AND A KICK OUT.

Mr. James O'Reilly, of the Sixteenth Ward, had heard with delight, as he always did, the words of the last speaker. But in one particular he thought that gentleman wrong. The national Democracy, led by such men as John McKeon, John Kelly, Brady, Van Buren, and Richard O'Gorman, could neither be sneered nor pooh-poohed out of existence. The impression that their organization was not a strong one, he regretted to be obliged to say, was wrong. They had the bone and sinew of the party, as well as nearly all its respectability and talent. Men like Red-Headed Tom Ferris, one of the gamest boys that lived; Ben Ray, Sheriff Lynch, Mat Gooderson, Isaiah Rynders, and James Irving, were not to be despised. He was sure——

Mr. Jake Sharp hereupon rose, and furiously demanded the instant expulsion of Mr. James O'Reilly, which had been already carried unanimously—the Duke of Bloomingdale, the senior representative of West Washington market, and Mr. P. Griese voting in the affirmative, and the chairman thereupon declaring it to be the ascertained will of the whole meeting. (Loud applause.) The Chairman would add that if any one could say that he had seen any other man look approbation while Mr. J. O'Reilly was speaking, the person who had dared so to look should also be expelled. (Dead silence.)

JIMMY NESBITT'S SONG.

Mr. Nesbitt here jumped up on one of the benches, and said he had a song so pat to James O'Reilly's case, that with the permission of the chair and those present, he'd be glad to give it to them. This proposal was hailed with deafening shouts—for Jimmy Nesbitt is a good fellow and a popular favorite; and, when quiet was restored, thus Jimmy sang, and with immense effect, the following verses, which the chairman announced to be by Private Miles O'Reilly, Forty-seventh regiment New York Volunteers, who only remained away in deference to the fact that, belonging as yet to the army—his discharge not having arrived, though hourly expected—he could not take part in a political meeting:—

Arrah! tare and 'ages,
How the haythen rages;
An' how the people do think foolish things!
They grip an' shake us,
In the hope to make us
Give up our big "bones" in the lobby "rings,"

'Tis because they're jealous—
All them outside fellows;
But, faix! we know betther, an' we'll hould our own;
Och, about the "moral"
Let the docthors quarrel;
But there's not one of us—no, not for St. Pathrick wid
Father Matthew to back him—that will give up our "bone."

Faix, from every steeple
You may call the people,
Wid both bell an' thrumpet, for to put us down;
But you'll only rue it,
For you'll fail to do it;
Och, our three machines, boys, they conthrols the town!
Don't breed a riot,
Just submit in quiet;
The more you sthruggle you'll be licked the worse;
An' the min you fought for,
That you worked and thought for,
When you're down in the gutther—havin' been run over by the
machines you thried to stop—they won't care a curse.

Some people wondher,
Whin they see the plundher
That is goin' on daily in full public view,
That the town don't rise up,
Fix a hundhred ties up,
An' do some lynchin' on the godless crew?

But we say, to the divil
Wid all such dhrivel,
The machines is mighty, an' they can't be beat;
So let's all "go in," boys;
'Tis the way to win, boys;
And let every mother's son o' you own a railroad, or two or three, if that will suit him any betther, in his private sthreet.

In the "market" line, boys,
There are pickin's fine, boys,
If you're only started on the inside thrack;
There are sinecure places,
An' there's ferry lases
That can make you nabobs in a single crack!
Or commince to liti-
Gate aginst the city:
There's no road to fortune that's so quick an' "Sharp"—
Faix, I've seen it thried, boys;
An' don't seek to hide, boys,
That the money comes in that way just as aisy, if not a little aisier, than playin' at "head an' harp."

A REPUBLICAN MACHINE-VIEW OF THE MACHINE.

The senior Republican representative of West Washington market now wished to call the attention of the Chair and of all present to the very beautiful and accurate model of the city of New York, which had been thoughtfully laid before them, just as coroners expose a dead body to the jury before proceeding with their inquest. The model on the stage was a political model of the great city in which they lived and were prospering. ("Hear, hear.") An examination of its proportions would show them why and how they prospered, and the importance of keeping all the existing machines in control. In this model, the shanties of Mackerelville, they would observe, were as large as the finest mansions between Highbridge and the Battery. This was because they held as many votes. A single tenement house in the "Dead Rabbit" district of the Sixth ward counted more votes than one whole side of Madison square. (Loud cheers.) The humbler classes, he was happy to say, had never been taught their own interests in public matters. They cared nothing about taxation, believing that their landlords had to pay it. The rich cared little either, knowing that all they paid would come out of the pockets of their tenants, and with interest. Tax Mr. Wm. B. Astor an extra ten thousand dollars a year, and he will only add it to his rents. All taxation is paid in the last resort by the very poorest. Overtax the merchant, and he meets it by dismissing some of his clerks and making the others work harder and later. Overtax the manufacturer, and he reduces the wages of his operatives. Everywhere the burden is shifted from shoulder to shoulder until you come down at last to the very humblest strata, and on them perforce it rests. (Loud cheers.) And this, fortunately for the politicians, has never been explained to the poor. When their rents are raised, they curse their landlords; when their wages are reduced, they curse their employers: and it never seems to occur to them—and here he thought was the richest part of the joke—that their own votes last year, and the year before, and the year before that again, were at the bottom of all their sufferings. (Loud laughter, mingled with applause.)

ANOTHER INTERRUPTION—MR. KERRIGAN WISHES TO "OPEN A LITTLE GAME."

Here there was a slight interruption, caused by a proposal from the Hon. J. C. Kerrigan that they should now "open a little game" for the judgeships, civil and police, which were to be disposed of in December. Mr. Kerrigan would either toss coppers, draw straws or play poker with any gentleman present for any one of the offices in question. As there were many candidates for these offices in the room, he thought that quite a handsome "pool" could be made up, if they were all ready and would check in.

The Chair called Mr. Kerrigan to order. The representative from West Washington market had the floor at present, and until he vacated it the proposition of the gentleman from the Sixth could not be entertained. When his Gansevoort friend was through, Mr. Kerrigan's proposition should receive all the attention to which it was entitled; but he believed that the Duke of Bloomingdale intended to dispose of such nominations as fell to him on behalf of Mozart Hall in a more business-like manner, and on more strictly commercial principles. So far as the Tammany nominations went, a raffle or game of poker might be in order.

FOUR SENATORS AND SEVENTEEN ASSEMBLYMEN WANTED.

The member from West Washington and Fort Gansevoort then resumed:—In such company it was not necessary to dwell upon the very complex system of "strings" and "wires" by which the whole city was dominated from the City Hall. (Hear, hear.) They all understood it. They were all growing rich by it, and would yet grow richer. (Loud applause.) He would call their attention, however, to the masterstroke of the whole machine. The cable of four thicker and seventeen thinner strands, connecting the network of the City Government with Albany, was typical of the part played in the construction and management of this mechanism by the majority of Senatorial and Assembly representatives who had been sent from Manhattan Island to Albany during the last half dozen years. (Cheers.) He would not name them, but would let "expressive silence muse their praise." (Cheers and laughter.) He hoped this year that they might be enabled to send up the river —he did not mean to Sing Sing, but to Albany—four Senators and seventeen Assemblymen of the best possible stripe. It only needed the election of the Lobby League Candidates for Senate and Assembly to fully enable them to carry out the proposition of the distinguished soldier, Private Miles O'Reilly, on whose call they were assembled. He thought that these candidates were only next in importance to Judges of the right stripe, and on these they were determined.

A BUSH WITH A BIRD IN IT TALKED ABOUT.

Here a rumor reached the hall that Private Miles O'Reilly was down stairs, and would be up in a few minutes, carrying a holly bush in his hand, and in the bush a mocking bird from South Carolina. This announcement created wild and uproarious applause, with cries of "Let Miles speak next," "Let the boy tell his own story," "Three cheers for the 'Bird in the Bush,'"* and so forth.

CONTROLLING VIEWS PUT FORTH.

Mr. John H. Doty believed he had some control in this concern, and he would like to see any one dare to interrupt him. He had the power, and would use it. He was no sentimentalist, but had a heart. All knew the sacrifices he had made for certain "next friends" who should be nameless. They were men who were—like the corporators in the Broadway Railroad—unknown to fame, unknown even to the Directory. But he was their "friend," and was always ready to do his utmost in their favor. Thanks to special legislation by former Republican Legislatures in behalf of one of their own pets, he held control over the machines of all parties, and would hold it for several years. All the boasted wire arrangements of the model were very fine; but did they not see that every wire out of the many thousands traversing the city and running to its "placers," had in the

* This was the signature to certain letters on local Democratic Politics published in the N. Y. Times six years ago.

final stage before fruition to pass under his control? He did not care to expose at once how absolute was the power which special legislation had placed in his hands. As the occasion rose, he would use the power; and before another year every public man and every newspaper* in the city should either bow to his dictation or be crushed. He was not a refined man and he never minced matters. It was important to him that Judges of the right stripe, four Senators of the right stripe, two Supervisors of the right stripe, seventeen Assemblymen of the right stripe, a Mayor of the right stripe, eight Aldermen of the right stripe, twenty-four Councilmen of the right stripe, and all the Police and Civil Justices of the right stripe should be elected, and he was decidedly in favor of the "Joint Stock Consolidated Lobby League." (Loud Cheers.) He thought Private O'Reilly's proposition for an absorption by the politicians of all the property of the city, real and personal, in four years, a most excellent one; but it was not original, as he could prove. He and some few friends had been working on the same idea for fifteen or twenty years. He favored the proposal made by the bard of Morris Island, that the stockholders in the political company should at the right moment

* An allusion, doubtless, to his large advertising patronage.

commence cheating each other; and finally he would propose, and was ready to expel every one who objected, that certain "next friends" whom he would name at the right time, should be made the recipients of the final "consolidation of interests" which was embraced in Private O'Reilly's very statesmanlike and equitable plan.

M'KEON'S DEMOCRACY ON THE WAR PATH—CHILLED GLASS AND HOT WATER—KICKED CURS AND BITING MASTIFFS.

Mr. John Kelly, who was one of the few dozen respectables who had come in to look at this curious gathering, had a few words to say. He knew he had friends enough in the crowd to protect him. The last speaker, he confessed, talked too dictatorially to suit his democratic nerves. That the position which Mr. Doty held was a goblet of immense dimensions he would not deny. It had been enlarged and enlarged by special legation, until there was no knowing how much it did or could contain. Probably, however, it held more power than any one man could quaff without danger of losing his balance. Such goblets fortunately were of chilled glass. Ten drops of scalding truth would shiver them into atoms. Men who kept cur dogs at their heels used their feet freely. Some day they would kick a mastiff, and then be taught the difference. He was happy to say that some friends of his, who were large stockholders in the "Consolidated Stage Company," had at length got a majority of the stock of that concern, and were about to sue for the turning over to the company of all shares in City Railroad Bills granted by former legislatures to individuals who represented themselves to be the agents and attorneys of that company. (Suppressed cheers.) Powerful as Mr. Doty and his friends might eventually become when they had all their own Judges on the bench, stronger combinations had been broken, and would be again. (Suppressed but increasing applause.) They did not yet own all the judiciary; and there was still upon the bench——[The remainder of the speech was drowned in hisses, cheers, and much confusion.]

PETER IN A PECK OF TROUBLE—HE BECOMES RUMBUNCTIOUS.

Mr. Griese was filled with disgust and loathing as he contemplated the speckled and miserable vulture who had just been addressing them. Such atrocious sentiments were insurrectionary. He moved that all present who were not adherents of the dominant dynasty, and who could either read or write, should be expelled. (Loud cheers.) It should be his peculiar privilege, he claimed, to do all the reading and writing of the whole concern. He insisted that both the dividends voted by the Company, to which the last speaker had the impudence to refer, were legitimately expended; and that all he had received from the Legislature was no more than fair compensation for his time and labor. The widows and orphans who held stock in that Company shonld have looked out for themselves, as he had done. He had been their agent just up to the passage of the different bills; but his agency ceased immediately preceding the passage, and his name or that of his dummy, in each bill, represented only his private interest.

MR. SHARP DOES NOT DESPISE THE DAY OF SMALL THINGS.

Mr. Sharp was in favor of having peace in the family, almost at any price. If they quarrelled among themselves their enemies, the proverb said, might come by their own. He thought they need not grasp everything at once. If they could gain one Judge a year, it would not be doing badly. Some Judges could not make the decisions they might want, but would be willing to acquiesce made by their bolder associates. This suited him well enough, and he thought should suit others. He had been in the business more than twenty years, and never saw things, with good management, looking so prosperous as now. His friends should not urge matters too far. They should be reasonable in their demands, and divide fair. One Judge a year would do him. [Applause, and cries of "Be sure you get it."]

REFORM MOVEMENTS "ALL A FARCE."

Mr. Alderman Farley was not afraid of public opinion. They had seen "reform movements" before, and knew how they resulted. Always heretofore, they had put men better suited to their purposes into power. "Reform movements" drew to them two classes amongst politicians—the men turned out of existing "machines" as not worth their pay and rations. This was one class. The other class was that of well-meaning but imbecile noodles, who meant to do strictly right, but knew not enough to prevent their being dragged this way and that by adroit schemers.—If a "reform movement" should fall into the hands of men upright, experienced and active—then, indeed, there would be danger. But this, he believed, could never happen. The men they might really fear were too noble to engage in the business.

MR. GEO. WILKES TALKS OF A VIGILANCE COMMITTEE.

Mr. Wilkes wished the Alderman not to be too sure of that. The so-called "reform movements," which had resulted in impotence, were bogus reform movements, in which the people took no interest. They were the mere result of intrigues or caucusings amongst "soreheads" of the class which the Alderman had so well described. But he (Mr. Geo. Wilkes) had been present at one popular "reform movement" in which the people were interested, and he could assure them it was a terribly earnest thing. He referred to the grand reform association, known as the San Francisco Vigilance Committee. (Deep sensation, and much uneasiness, many moving towards the door.) He saw they had heard of it. It was an association, which had violated all law, in order to obtain substantial justice, after every other means had failed. (Sensation increasing.) Should such a "reform movement" as that ever break out or be organized in the city of New York, he would advise nine-tenths of the present assemblage to be out of town while the reformers were on the war path.

CLOSING SPEECH BY THE CHAIR.

The sensation made by this speech can more easily be imagined than described. Cheers, hootings, applause, yells and screams broke out in one mingled uproar. The representatives of the three "regular machines" whispered eagerly with the Chairman for a few moments, and then disappeared. The Chairman himself declared hurriedly that the caucus stood adjourned until further notice. Its proceedings had been satisfactory and harmonious to a degree never before witnessed. As he understood matters, all present had agreed to place their interests in the hands of the three regular Tammany, Mozart and Republican representatives, who had just departed with their immediate friends; while, as for himself, he would take care of himself, and hoped they might all be as successful. The "blue lights," he would remind them, were burning low, and he called upon such members of the police as might be present to see that the very valuable and curious model of their new "machine," containing in its proportions, and the net-work of its wires and strings, all the secrets of the "Joint Stock Consolidated Grand Junction Lobby League," should suffer no injury. He would now say good night.

CONCLUSION OF THE MILES O'REILLY CAUCUS.

No sooner had the burly figure of the Chairman quitted the stage than scores of profane feet leaped upon it, and hundreds of curious eyes examined for the first time that "machine," upon which only the most deeply initiated should ever be permitted to gaze. Among the crowd of amazed spectators, who had attended the caucus as "outsiders" and from a desire to see the "ruling classes of the city in council assembled," your reporter noticed scores of our really great and prominent men, whose names are familiar as household words in connexion with every enterprise which has lent grandeur, wealth, or dignity to the Empire City. They now gazed for the first time upon "the machine;" first saw exposed the system of trickery and fraud by which the treasury is depleted and the chevaliers of politics enriched. It was a sight to move deep thought in the breast of every reflective and intelligent man, whose destinies are cast in with the fortunes of Manhattan Island. Is that machine to dominate for ever? Shall the programme of the managing leaders be carried out? Is there no way by which, in one united effort, the sceptre of this political Moloch can be broken? Evidently the cable linking the city mechanism to Albany should be sundered at any cost. Evidently the Judges most obnoxious to the managing leaders of the "machine" are those who should be elected. But to do all this will require some sacrifices. It may take time. The machine, as depicted in the model, is the work of many years. It may take a year, it may take more, to break it. Are there enough good men and true in the city of New York to make one effort to this end? If there be not, then let the machines run on until all the purposes of the leading spirits of this caucus have been fully and triumphantly accomplished! Men, who will do nothing to save themselves, are not worth saving. Many who sat down to read this expected a farce, and they have found a sermon. The subject is too serious to be trifled with; for—

Vain is irony ; unmeet
  Its polished words for deeds which start
In fiery and indignant beat
  The pulses of the heart.

CHAPTER IX.

MILES O'REILLY AT THE WHITE HOUSE.

[From the N. Y. Herald.]

WASHINGTON, Nov. 26, 1863.

LET to-day be chronicled as a great day for Ireland, and let it live as the greatest of Thanksgiving Days in American history! This afternoon took place the interesting ceremonial of presenting Private Miles O'Reilly, Forty-seventh Regiment New York Volunteers, to his Excellency the President of the United States, by whom, in turn, the young Milesian warrior and bard of the Tenth army corps was presented to several members of the Cabinet and foreign diplomatic corps, who were paying a Thanksgiving Day call to the President when the cards of General T. F. Meagher and Father Murphy were handed in by Colonel Hay—these gentlemen having kindly consented to act as the *chaperons*, or social godfathers and godmothers of Private O'Reilly, who was accompanied by Major Kavanagh and Captain Breslin, of the old Sixty-ninth New York, and by Mr. Luke Clark, of the Fifth Ward of your City, as his own "special friends." The details of this interview will hereafter form an instructive episode in the grand drama of our national history. It was in a manner the apotheosis of democratic principles—an acknowledgment of our indebtedness to the men who carry muskets in our armies. It had its political significance, also, and may prove another link between our soldiers in the field and the present lengthy occupant of the White House, who is understood to be not averse to the prospect of a lengthier lease of that "desirable country residence," which has none of the modern improvements.

PICTURE OF PRIVATE O'REILLY.

Private O'Reilly is a brawny, large-boned, rather good-looking young Milesian, with curly reddish hair, grey eyes, one of which has a blemish upon it, high cheek bones, a cocked nose, square lower jaws, and the usual strong type of Irish forehead—the perceptive bumps, immediately above the eyes, being extremely prominent. A more good-humored or radiantly expressive face it is impossible to conceive. The whole countenance beams with a candor and unreserve equal to that of a mealy potato which has burst its skin or jacket by too rapid boiling. He stands about six feet three inches, is broad-chested, barrel-bodied, firm on his pins, and with sinewy, knotted fists of a hardness and heaviness seldom equalled. On the whole, he reminds one very much of Ensign O'Doherty's ideal picture of the Milesian hero:—

One of his eyes was bottle green,
And the other eye was out, my dear;
And the calves of his wicked looking legs
Were more than two feet about, my dear!
O, the lump of an Irishman,
The nasty, ugly Irishman,
The great he-rogue, with his wonderful brogue,
The leathering swash of an Irishman.

WHAT HE AND HIS COUSINS THINK ABOUT ENGLAND.

Private O Reilly says that he was born at a place they call Ouldcastle; that he picked up what little of the humanities and rudiments he possesses under one Father Thomas Maguire, of Cavan—"him that was O'Connell's frind, rest their sowls;" and he is emphatic in declaring that he and seventeen of his O'Reilly cousins, sixty-four Murphy cousins, thirty-seven Kelly cousins, twenty-three Lanigan cousins, together with a small army of Raffertys, Caffertys, Fogartys, Flanigans, Ryans, O'Rourkes, Dooligans, Oulahans, Quinns, Flynns, Kellys, Murphys, O'Connors, O'Connells, O'Driscolls, O'Mearas, O'Tooles, McCartys, McConkeys, and McConnells—all his own blood relations, many of them now in the service, and all decent boys—would be both proud and happy to enlist or re-enlist for twenty years or the war, if his Reverence's Excellency the President would only oblige them "the laste mite in life" by declaring war against England. He is of opinion that no excuse is ever needed for going to war; but adds that if any were, it might be found in the recent Canadian-rebel conspiracy to release the prisoners in camp on Johnson's Island.

"If we let this pass," he says, "divil resayve the so illigant an excuse the dirty spalpeens may ever give us again! They gripped us whin we wor wake, an' med us give up them two rapparees, Shlidell and Mason. We've now got five iron-clads to their one, boys dear; and Mr. Lincoln," he adds, "won't be the jockey he bought him for, if he don't give John Bull his bellyful of 'neuthrality' before he gets through his term." Mr. Luke Clark, of the Fifth ward, is understood to be very strong in the same view.

ARRIVAL AT THE WHITE HOUSE—SCENES AT THE DOOR.

On the arrival of the party at the White House there was a great scene of handshaking at the door between Private O'Reilly and Edward McManus, the chatty old greyhaired gentleman from Italy—where O'Reilly knew him—who has kept watch at the gate through five administrations; and who is now assisted by Mr. Thomas Burns, also from Italy, who has outlived the storms of two reigns. It was "God bless you, Miles," and "God bless you kindly, Edward," for as many as ten minutes, the handshaking being fast and furious all the time.

GENERAL MEAGHER'S SPEECH.

General Meagher, in presenting Private O'Reilly to the President, made some remarks to the effect that he was happy to have the honor of introducing to one who was regarded as the Father of the Army this *enfant perdu*, or lost boy of the Irish race. His friend, Colonel John Hay, the President's Secretary, who had served as a volunteer in the Department of the South, was acquainted with O'Reilly's character in his regiment, and knew that it was good, though chequered with certain amiable indiscretions, having their origin in the fount of Castaly, or some other fountain—of which he had forgotten the particulars. (Laughter.) He wished to assure Mr. Lincoln that the bone and sinew of the army—his own countrymen in it not least—had eyes to see, and hearts to feel, and memories to treasure up the many acts of hearty, homely, honest kindliness, by which the Chief Magistrate of the nation had evinced his interest in their welfare. In the golden hours of sunrise, under the silver watches of the stars, through many a damp, dark night on picket duty, or in the red flame and heady fury of the battle, the thought that lay next the heart of the Irish soldier—only dividing its glow with that of the revered relic from the altar, which piety and affection had annexed, as an amulet against harm, around his neck—was the thought that he was thus earning a title, which hereafter no foul tongue or niggard heart would dare dispute, to the full equality and fraternity of an American citizen. ("Hear, hear," from the President.) Ugly and venomous as was the toad of civil strife, it yet carried in its head for the Irish race in America this precious, this inestimable jewel. By adoption of the banner, and by the communion of bloody grave-trenches on every field, from Bull Run to where the

Chickamauga rolls down its waters of death, the race that were heretofore only exiles, receiving generous hospitality in the land, are now proud peers of the proudest and brave brothers of the best. (Deep emotion, Secretary Seward tapping the table with his fingers, and Mr. Chase gravely bowing his head in approval.) On behalf of Private O'Reilly, he desired to thank Mr. Lincoln for the clemency which had failed to see crime in an innocent song. Although the verses of Private O'Reilly had become conspicuous, they were far from being the only or the best efforts of the lyric muse to which the fast frolic and effervescing life of camps had given birth. Whenever Clio shall aspire to write the history of this war, that sagest sister of the sacred Nine will be obliged to draw largely on the rough, but always heartfelt, often droll, still oftener tenderly pathetic verses, with which Euterpe will be found to have inspired the rough writers and fighters of the rank and file. ("Hear, hear," from the President, the Baron Gerolte and General Cullum.) Seeing that Lord Lyons was present, General Meagher would not now refer to the Fenian Brotherhood, of which the Chevalier John O'Mahony was the Head Centre. He thanked the President, Mr. Seward, Mr. Chase, Mr.

Stanton, General Halleck, the Baron Stoeckl, the Baron Gerolte, the Count Mercier, Colonels Townsend and Kelton, Assistant Secretary of the Navy Fox, and the others who were present, for their interest in this interview, of which accident had made them witnesses. Had he had the slightest inkling how his Excellency had been engaged, he should most certainly have postponed the visit—a wish for which had been conveyed to him through Secretary Stanton. He would now briefly introduce to the President Private Miles O'Reilly, the bard of Morris Island, whose self and family—snug farmers and very decent people—he had well known many years ago in the Green Isle, which was their common birthplace.

MR. LINCOLN'S SPEECH—HIS STORY ABOUT "THE WIDOW ZOLLICOFFER'S DARKEY."

Mr. Lincoln replied that he was happy to see Private O'Reilly, but did not care to make a set speech. In his position it was not wise to talk foolishly, and he would, therefore, but rarely talk at all. As to the "war for the succession," about which the *Herald* and Mr. Wendell Phillips appeared crazy, he would say some few words. Men oftenest betray and defeat themselves by over-anxiety to secure their object, just as the widow Zollicoffer's nigger did, away down in Bourbon county, when he had been eating her cranberry jam. (Laughter.) The widow, while making her jam, was called away to a neighbor who was about increasing the population. (Loud laughter.) "Sam, you rascal," she said, "you'll be eating my jam when I'm away." Sam protested he'd die first; but the whites of his eyes rolled hungrily towards the bubbling crimson. "See here, Sam," said the widow, taking up a piece of chalk, "I'll chalk your lips, and then on my return I'll know if you've eaten any." So saying, she passed her forefinger heavily over the thick lips of her darkey, holding the chalk in the palm of her hand, and not letting it touch him. Well, when she came back, Sam's lips were chalked a quarter of an inch thick, and she needed against him no other evidence. (Laughter.) Now, it is much the same about the Presidency. (Renewed mirth.) A good friend of mine declares that he wouldn't take it at any price; but his lips were thickly chalked when he came back from Ohio. (Great merriment, in which Mr. Chase joined heartily.) So were General Fremont's, out in Missouri, when he issued his "emancipation order;" and General Butler's were not only chalked, but had the jam on and had it thick. Secretary Seward once chalked very badly, but had given it up as of no use since his quarrel with Mr. Weed, machine proprietor of his own State. (Loud laughter.) Mingled chalk and jam might be seen on the lips of General Banks; while the same compound formed quite a paste around the orifice through which his good friend Governor Seymour supplied the wants of nature. (Roars of laughter.) He had never seen any chalk on the lips of Secretary Stanton or General Henry W. Halleck: but, with these exceptions, there was scarcely a man connected with the army who did not chalk his lips. (Continued mirth, the foreign diplomatic corps joining heartily.) He believed many of the generals would compromise for a brigadier's commission in the regular army; but these were matters too grave to be joked about. He would now introduce to all present Private Miles O'Reilly, of the Tenth army corps—an army corps which had done well under General Gillmore, having been magnificently disciplined by General Hunter—perhaps the very strictest field officer in the service. Mr. Lincoln conclude by bidding the bard of Morris Island welcome to the White House, at the same time extending his hand for a friendly shake.

HOW PRIVATE O'REILLY SHAKES HANDS.

All this time Private Miles O'Reilly, Forty-seventh regiment New York Volunteers, had been standing in the first position of a soldier—heels in, toes out, body rigid and perpendicular as a ramrod, and the little fingers of his open hands resting behind the side seams of his sky-blue inexpressibles. He had a twenty-five cent bouquet in the breast of his blue coat, and in his eyes that stolid expression or total want of expression which is imparted by the order—"eyes front." No sooner, however, did the President extend his hand than the sinews relaxed, and his countenance brightened up as if some crazy millionaire had suddenly offered to give him its face in gold for a twenty dollar greenback. Instantly he made the sound of spitting into the palm of his right hand, then raised the arm to its full height, and brought down his open palm against the Presidential palm with a report that rang through the council chamber as if one of the "torpedo devils" of Chief Engineer Stimers had been exploded by the concussion. He no doubt intended to say something extremely eloquent; but laboring, like Charles Lamb, under a bad stammer, his words came slowly and with pain, though of their earnestness the very difficulty with which they were uttered gave proof.

MR. LUKE CLARK AS A DOCTOR.

Mr. Luke Clark suggested that it was timorous the boy was; that his heart was too full, and the words bubbled up so quick to his tongue that they choked and killed each other—like an audience crowding out through the narrow doors of a theatre in which the cry of "fire" has been raised. If his Reverence's Excellency the President would only order up a jug of water, with no more whiskey in it than President Pierce took at the opening of the Crystal Palace—"just enough to kill the animalculæ"—Mr. Clark was of opinion that Miles would rapidly recover.

The order was given. Private Miles retired for a few moments into Mr. Nicolay's room, just outside the council chamber, from whence he soon returned, wiping his mouth with the cuff of his coat, gasping a little for breath, and with his whole face so much brighter and livelier that it was like a transfiguration.

"Your Riverence's Excellency," he said, scraping his left foot backwards, bowing forward his body, and giving one of his red forelocks a jerk between the finger and thumb of his right hand: "Your Riverence's Excellency, though I'm wipin' my lips, it's nayther chalk nor cranberries I had on them last." (Loud laughter.)

LORD LYONS ASKS FOR A SONG—THE CABINET "POKING FUN."

"Suppose, Mr. Seward, you ask your young friend to give us a song," said Lord Lyons, who had been looking rather superciliously at all parts of the ceremonial. "They say the fellow can sing; and I suppose it is because he can sing, he is here."

Mr. Seward referred the matter by a bow to the President, who glanced sharply at Lord Lyons. For one moment a cloud passed over Mr. Lincoln's kindly face, but disappeared as he turned and let his eyes rest on the beaming countenance of Private Miles.

"What say you, Private O'Reilly? Will you sing?"

"I will that, your Riverence's Excellency," was the response, with just one flash of a scowl towards Lord Lyons. "It's my prayer for your Excellency that you may never die until the skin of a gooseberry makes a nightcap for you; and may you have the vigor of Lord Palmershin—that's your boss, Lord

Lyons—till the day you're a hundhred an' fifty!" (Uproarious laughter, in which all joined except Father Murphy—Lord Lyons laughing the loudest.) "Now, what shall I sing?" continued Private Miles. "If his Riverence, Father Pathrick Murphy, worn't to the fore, it's a song in honor of my counthryman, the same Lord Palmershin, that I'd give you. 'Tisn't that I ever loved him or any other anti-Irish Irishman, who takes blood money for the life of his counthry. (Sensation.) But it's because I'm sick of the humbug that is in them English journals that say the ould man ought to be ashamed of himself. (Laughter.) Faix, at his age, I can't see any shame about it. (Loud laughter.)

"*Au contraire*," suggested Count Mercier, with a smile and shrug: "*à son age, devrait au moins en être fier.*"

(Roars of laughter, amidst which Father Murphy retired in company with Mr. Nicolay, Colonel Hay's colleague, on the plea that the room was growing too hot for him.)

"How old do you say he is, my Lord?" said Secretary Seward, removing the cigar from his mouth.

"Old enough to be your father," was the reply; "he will be eighty next June." (Renewed laughter.)

THE DECANTERS AND THINGS ORDERED IN—COUNCIL TABLE CLEARED FOR A JOLLIFICATION—"GRANT'S PARTICULAR."

General Halleck here arose to suggest that now, while Father Murphy was absent, was the proper time, if ever, for the improper song.

"Col. Hay, please touch the bell," said Mr. Lincoln, "and let Burgdorf, my messenger, send us up the decanters and things. I have some French wines, sent me from Paris by Secretary of Legation Pennington, whose tongue is so completely occupied in the business of tasting vintages that he has never had time to teach it French, though a resident in Paris many years. If you prefer whiskey, I have some that can be relied upon—a present from Mr. Leslie Combs. I call it 'Grant's Particular,' and Halleck is about issuing an order that all his generals shall drink it."

"With the news we have to-day from Chattanooga," said Gen. Halleck, gaily, "I think the country will endorse the order to which Mr. Lincoln has referred. For my own part I'll take some of that whiskey—just enough to drown a mosquito, Kelton—and, with the President's permission, our first toast will be, the health of Ulysses Grant, the river-horse of the Mississippi!"

Secretary Stanton seconded the toast in a neat and spirited address, Mr. Lincoln frequently applauding. The health was received with all the honors, every one present standing up while the liquor went down, and the company giving three cheers for General Grant, and then three more, and then three after that to top off with.

Some drank it in wine, others whiskey. The council table was hastily cleared of books, papers, and maps. All took seats except Private O'Reilly, who continued to have spasms of rigidity and the "first position of a soldier" whenever his eyes happened to rest for a moment on General Halleck's buttons in bunches of three, or General Cullum's twin-button brigadier arrangement.

"Excuse me, gentlemen; this is my only beverage," said the President, filling out a glass of water. "Help yourselves. Seward, the diplomatic body is under your care. Baron Gerolte's glass is empty. General Meagher, will you be kind enough to see what the friends of Private O'Reilly will take? Now, Miles, clear your throat with a glass of wine—not too much for him, Colonel

Hay—and let us hear your song in honor of Lord Palmerston."

Private O'Reilly tossed off a *demitasse*, and then gave, with irresistible drollery and a really fine baritone voice, the following words, to the well known air, once so popular in the mouth of John Brougham —" Ould Ireland You're My Darling."

LORD PALMERSTON AND MRS. O'KANE.

Of all the min wid swoord or pin
  Who live in song or story,
'Till time lets pass his empty glass,
  Lord Pam, 'tis you're my glory;
And this shall be the song for me,
  As years are o'er me flowin'—
Time take all else, but lave my pulse
  Like Pam's as warmly glowin'!
Chorus—Of all the min wid swoord or pin
    Who live in Irish story,
  Till time lets pass his empty glass,
    Lord Pam—[ye ould sinner, wid your wicked arts, your white head and your everlastin' physique]
  Lord Pam, 'tis you're my glory!

To Mrs. O'Kane a glass we dhrain,
  In silks we will attire her;
And Cromwell's curse, or somethin' worse
  On the dunce that don't admire her!

Fresh, fair, and young, Pam's winnin' tongue
Gev argyment so weighty,
That Parson O'Kane she quitted wid pain
For a lover hard on to eighty.
Chorus—Och! of all the pearls of precious girls
That live in song or story,
Wid Vaynus' art to fire the heart,
[Mrs. O'Kane, my jewel—Mrs. O'Kane, *acushla*—Mrs. O'Kane, *mavourneen dheelish, asthore macree*]
'Tis you, 'tis you're my glory!

Lord Pam is great, a shpaker nate,
Britannia's frisky ruler;
In high debate on pints of shtate
No head than his is cooler;
But undhernathe the silvery wrathe—
Ould Time's white frost or ashes—
Like Etna's fire, his heart's desire
Breaks out in tindher flashes.
Chorus—Of all the min wid swoord or pin,
Who live in British story,
Till time lets pass his empty glass,
Lord Pam—[*Avic!*—ye ould deludherer, that ought to know betther, and that does know betther, but can't help yourself, *aroon*]—
Lord Pam, 'tis you're my glory!

There's somethin' quare in Irish air
And a diet of pitaties,
That makes us all so prone to fall

To whishkey and the ladies;
Wid these galore, what want we more,
Our heads are wildly turnin';
While in our flood of dancin' blood
Delight is fairly burnin'.
Chorus—But of all the min wid swoord or pin,
Who live in the wide world's story,
Till time lets pass his empty glass,
Lord Pam—[An' bad 'cess to me if you can't have half my rations, half my tent, and half my canteen any day in the year]
Lord Pam, 'tis you're my glory!

So pledge the toast, Britannia's boast,
His sthrongest wakeness pardon;
And let no thrick, my royal Vic,
Your heart aginst him harden!
The warmest vein has clearest brain,
The proofs are sthrong and weighty;
So to Mrs. O'Kane a glass we'll dhrain,
And to Pam, her lover of eighty!
Chorus—Och, of all the pearls of precious girls,
An' of all the lovers hoary,
Till time lets pass his empty glass,
Lord Pam—[And you, Mrs. O'Kane, dear, that's able to illecthrify a telegraph post wid one wink of your rollickin' eye, *acushla*]
Yez both, dears, are my glory!

HOW THE SONG WAS RECEIVED.

To describe the roars of laughter with which this lyric was received, would be impossible, his Reverence's Excellency the President alone preserving an immovable countenance. Seward was in convulsions. Chase lost much of that dignified deportment, showing elevation of character as well as of position, for which he has been remarked. Stanton was purple, and pressed his left hand on his side to check the pain of excessive merriment. The diplomatic body, in various stages of exhaustion, begged Mr. Lincoln to stop the song, or it would be the death of them. Halleck shook a strong rosewood arm-chair, in which he sat, nearly to bits, the tears rolling down his swarthy cheeks, and his black eyes glittering with an intensity of humorous relief. Secretary Welles, when it was over, first carefully picked up several of his waistcoat buttons from the floor, and then put on his spectacles to examine with due deliberation what manner of man Private Miles might be; after which he declared that the song was "one of the most interesting he had heard for many years!"

MR. LINCOLN OPENS THE BALL—HE THINKS MRS. O'KANE A VERY SERIOUS MATTER.

His Excellency the President, who had been sitting, curled up in an arm-chair, with his legs loosely crossed one over the other, now began to rise, slowing untwisting the kinks of his back, and towering up like one of the genii, or afrites, released from the jar, or jug, in which they had been bottled up for centuries under the seal of Solomon.

"Aisy!" exclaimed Mr. Luke Clark, with unaffected dismay. "It's dashin' your brains out agin the ceilin' you'll be, or tanglin' your shouldhers in the top notches of the shandyleer!"

At length, Mr. Lincoln reached his full height, and said, that he had not quite caught the drift of the song; but from what little of it he did catch, it was just as well that he had caught no more.

"Hear, hear," from Father Murphy, who had re-entered the room during the singing of the last four lines.

Being on friendly terms with Great Britain, Mr. Lincoln continued, he trusted that the song would go no further.

"Hear, hear," from Lord Lyons, who was trying

O'REILLY IN THE PRESENCE CHAMBER—Page 174.

hard to smother some refluent waves of laughter.

"There are themes," continued Mr. Lincoln—"and Mrs. O'Kane is one of them—much too serious to be joked about." With this admonition, made as gentle as he could, he would now ask Private O'Reilly's opinion as to how the next Presidency was going?

PRIVATE O'REILLY ON THE SUCCESSION.

Private O'Reilly's stammer immediately became very bad again, insomuch that Colonel Hay, remembering the successful treatment previously recommended, had to administer, but only as a medicine, another small dose of some amber-hued beverage.

"I think," said Private Miles, when he had recovered his breath, and again wiped his lips with his coat cuff: "I think that the politicianers is all wrong about it, your Riverence's Excellency; and there's not the humblest gossoon in the army to-day, that couldn't tell them more than they know on that subject, wid all their caucussings and convintions."

"Well, explain," said Mr. Chase, rather anxiously, but still preserving all his *aplomb* of manner and gracious courtesy of smile.

"They could tell them," said Private Miles, "that there's but one man who wears a Black Coat in the United States this blessed and holy day, that can be elected to that office. Mind, I'm not sayin'—for I'm no flattherer, and I'm no seventh son—that he will be. All I do say is, that there's only one Black Coat in the Union, that can be a successful candydate for that office."

HOW THE SOLDIERS WILL VOTE.

"You think blue, with brass buttons, the healthiest color for Presidential aspirants to appear in," queried Mr. Seward, casting a sly glance as he spoke from under his shaggy gray eyebrows in the direction of Secretary Chase.

"Faix, sir, you might sing that same, if you knew any tune that would fit it," was Private O'Reilly's answer. "Every Presidential candidate should appear in blue an' goold, the way Ticknor and Fields publishes their pocket editions of the poicks. There's half a million of us that can vote, though Governor Saymour won't let any of us New York boys vote by proxy; and it's for no black coat in the Union, except one, that the army vote will be given. Everything depinds now on how the war goes. It may be

Grant, and it will be Grant, if his gallant victhories continue; or it may be Dix, who is very sthrong wid all classes; or it may be Banks, who will have the New England States solid; or it may be Rosy, whose devotions have touched the thrue Church; or, last of all, if the war goes well as a whole, Gineral Halleck will be an almighty hard man to defeat before a dimmycratic convintion. The very fact that he has held back, and hasn't been curryin' favor anywhere, will be the strongest card in his hand. Of Gineral McClellan I say nothin', for the proper time hasn't come yet—except that those who think he's played out, may find themselves mistaken some fine mornin'. There'll be milithary candydates as plenty as thorns on a brier bush, or black feathers on a crow. Aginst the canvass of votes in your big cities, will be the votes of our canvass towns. The boys who for the last two years and more have been carryin' their butchery, bakery, and grocery in a haversack over one hip, and their tavern in a canteen over the other, will all vote just as they have been taught to fight—facin' the same way, and touchin' the elbow. I hear people sayin' that this gineral is shtrong wid the Germans, and that some other gineral is shtrong with the Irish; but I tell you that there's nayther Irish nor Germans amongst the min who have been atin', marchin', shleepin' an' fightin' side by side since the summer that was two years ago. If it would be agreeable to this noble company, who are the very hoigth of quality, there was a song that was wrote to illusthrate this subjeck, which he'd as soon sing as not. It was wrote by Gineral Isaac I. Stevens—God rest his sowl!—who was killed near Centhreville—more's the pity—his son dhroppin' badly wounded from his horse just as a rifle ball whistled through the father's forehead."

Private O'Reilly's voice grew rather husky towards the close of this address, and his eyes were suffused with an unusual moisture. Clearing his throat at length by an effort which was half a cough, half sob, he sang the following words amidst deep silence on the part of his audience, to the air of "Jamie's on the Stormy Sea:"

SONG OF THE SOLDIERS.

Comrades known in marches many,
Comrades tried in dangers many,
Comrades bound by memories many,
  Brothers ever let us be!
Wounds or sickness may divide us,
Marching orders may divide us,
But, whatever fate betide us,
  Brothers of the heart are we.

Comrades known by faith the clearest,
Tried when death was near and nearest,
Bound we are by ties the dearest,
  Brothers ever more to be :—
And, if spared and growing older,
Shoulder still in line with shoulder,
And with hearts no thrill the colder,
  Brothers ever we shall be.

By communion of the banner—
Battle-scarred but victor banner,
By the baptism of the banner,
  Brothers of one church are we!
Creed nor faction can divide us,
Race nor language can divide us,
Still, whatever fate betide us,
  Children of the flag are we!

The deep and dead silence which followed this song was fully as flattering to Private O'Reilly's vocal powers as had been the tumultuous laughter which hailed his Lord Palmerston ditty. This "Song of the Soldiers" he gave with the greatest energy and enthusiasm, his chest swelling, his feet taking firmer stand on the floor, and his gray eyes kindling up with flashes of electric vivacity. None could doubt who heard and saw him, that in songs of this kind, and in the spirit which animates them, and amongst the men who feel them and are their subject, the future government of the United States is centred.

WHAT SAY THE PEOPLE?

"That's a gallant song," said the President, first breaking silence, and sighing as he spoke. "If I had heard it, and had known Ike Stevens wrote it, he should have had two stars on each shoulder before he died. But haven't you anything livelier, Miles? Mind, I don't mean liveliness of your Lord Palmerston type. Tell us, if you can, what the people say of us; what they say of Chase; what of Seward? You needn't be afraid, Miles: we ain't a thin-skinned family, and we know before asking that you have an awkward knack of telling the truth."

Private O'Reilly said he had no song to give them on this subject just now; but would be happy if they would hear a song from his friend Mr. Luke Clark, who had an excellent voice.

Mr. Clark said the song he was about to sing was one which he had picked up at a "free and easy," in a place they called the Ivy Green, which is a sort of chapel of ease to the Pewter Mug, and which is kept, he said, by Jim McGowan and Johnny Lord—

"two as square men as ever drew ale from tap, or whirled the mixer round in a temperance cocktail." Luke had been introduced there by his friend, Alderman Billy Walsh, of whose brother, the "King of the Dead Rabbits," Mr. Lincoln must have heard. The song he was about to give them had been sung there frequently by Senator Chris. Woodruff, a lucky boy, and had never failed to bring down the house. He hoped it would give offence to nobody.

MR. LUKE CLARK'S SONG.

With these brief prefatory remarks, Mr. Clark now cleared his throat, and sang, with a voice of stentorian power, the following ditty, to the well-known and lively air of "Nora Creina :—

A CABINET PHOTOGRAPH.

Stanton's beard is thick and long,
  And rough and tough his portly figure;
But his heart is brave and strong
  With fierce vitality and vigor.
Work that might a dozen men
  Tire to death, he knocks off gaily,
And, blundering badly now and then,
  Does true and noble service daily.

Oh, my Edwin, dread and dear,
Dispensing fount of pay and rations,
Private Miles upon you smiles,
"Conformably to Regulations."

Seward loves to smoke and dream,
Fit chief for theoretic faction;
Great to talk on every theme,
But failure flat in every action.
Aiming Abe to mould and bend,
On each associate's rights in ringing,
Lukewarm to the Czar—our friend—
And to John Bull most humbly cringing.
Oh, my Seward, since you changed
Your faith in Weed, your fate is dismal;
He and Greeley now estranged,
Before you yawns a pit abysmal.

Angular and lank and bare,
His whiskers, like his habits, foxy,
Forward steps Montgomery Blair,
Who throws his family vote by proxy.
Mistress Bates is next in line,
With poodle, bundles and umbrella;
Good old soul! whose gooseberry wine
Is, like her spirit, sweet and mellow.
Dear old lady—bless your heart,
Our love and reverence we accord you;
'Tis you that took Ike Fowler's part—
And for the act may Heaven reward you!

Then there's Uncle Gid, whose cast
 Of face inspires each artist's noddle;
When this cruel war is past
 They'll hire him as a "patriarch model."
Next is Usher, like a bat,
 Who aid to either winner offers—
Now a pigeon, now a rat—
 Twixt Chase and Blair he doubtful hovers.
  Oh, my Usher, hard to catch,
   As sinewy, slippery as a boa—
  While Gid, through Mrs. Cora Hatch,
   Is taught by Heaven's own Admiral, Noah!

Salmon hath a paper mill,
 Which night and day pursues its journey;
Soon with greenbacks he will fill
 The land from Maine to Califurny.
Oh, the vanished days of gold!
 The vanished, halcyon days of specie!
Bullion's dead, and coin has fled
 On paper winglets to Hel—vetia.
  Oh, my Chase, my Salmon dear
   My greenly gleaming, gorgeous Salmon,
  Down paper's tide serene you glide—
   A tide that hasn't got a dam on!

Grand and grim is Salmon's face
 While on financial themes he ponders;
Clear his eye, his bearing high,
 As in his greenback dreams he wanders.

Oh, could he but give us back
  The days ere paper did affright us,
Never should our Salmon lack
  Aquarial lodgings in the White House.
    Oh, my Chase, my Salmon dear,
      The country well may mourn in sables—
    Bullion's dead and coin has fled—
      Our cash consists of claret labels!

TERRIBLE EFFECTS OF "FREE SONG"—UNIVERSAL EXECRATION OF MR. CLARK.

The sudden dropping into the room of one of Gillmore's Greek fire three-hundred-pounders could not have produced greater consternation than the singing of this ditty—Private O'Reilly making several ineffectual motions to stop his blundering friend, who—sublimely unconscious of any impropriety—kept on singing with a force which recalled the historical roaring of the thousand bulls of Bashan. Every one felt as if a wet blanket or douche bath had been suddenly applied down his spine—Mr. Chase alone preserving all his stately urbanity, and beating time with his fingers on the elbow of his arm chair to the unfortunate melody. On the conclusion of the song, dead silence followed—some slight chucklings of Lord Lyons and the Count Mercier alone excepted. At this silence Mr. Luke Clark appeared deeply hurt, having apparently expected the same applause he had so often received for the same performance in less elevated latitudes. It was only when he saw General Meagher, with the greater part of his handkerchief stuffed down his throat, and Private O'Reilly, his face white with rage, shaking his fist at him in a highly belligerent manner, that Mr. Clark began to suspect it might be possible that he had been committing a *faux pas*—"puttin' his fut into it"—in his own vernacular.

"I have to apologize for my misfortunate frind," said Private Miles, stammering very badly. "It's little I thought the kind of song the divil would put it into his head to sing whin I axed him."

"Oh, all right," said the President, reassuringly. "We asked you to tell us what the people said of us, and your friend Clark has only been doing it with a vengeance."

AUTHORS AND CIRCULATORS OF THE SONG DENOUNCED.

General Meagher said that Irishmen were proverbial for blunders of all sorts, and this meeting would perhaps have been incomplete, bnt for the recent ludicrous incident. Nothing that the malice of enemies could put in verse, or that the ignorance of such men as Mr. Clark could be used to propagate, would injure that well earned and substantial fame which Mr. Chase's administration of the finan ces of the country had acquired. To the other injured members of the Cabinet he made similar soothing complimentary allusions.

Mr. Chase begged General Meagher to give himself no uneasiness about an incident which they would long remember as one of the most amusing of their official lives. He would only add that he had heard that song before, and that his friend Mr. George Wilkes reported it to have been written by Mr. Samuel L. M. Barlow, and put into circulation by a secret society for the diffusion of copperhead information, of which Mr. Hiram Cranston and C. Godfrey Gunther were the presiding officers. He felt that he need say no more.

In order to smoothe over the trifling interruption of good feeling which had taken place, Mr. Seward would suggest that Private O'Reilly should leave off his gestures and black looks against his friend, Mr. Clark, and give them another lyric—if he had one, another army song.

Private Miles declared himself so mortified by the

blunders of that omadhawn—nodding in the direction of Mr. Clark—that he had scarce any heart left to sing anything. The best he could do, however, he would; so he'd give them a song that was composed by his *soggarth*, Father Murphy, who had been chaplain, and a good one, God bless him! to the poor boys of the Irish Brigade, in the days of its hardest fights under General Meagher, who ought to have two stars on each shoulder, or there could be no such thing as justice to Ireland. He picked out this song, as it was about the army and the Presidency, two matters most likely to be of interest to the hearer to whom he owed gratitude for his pardon, and was most anxious to please. He then sang, with rising spirit, as his mind recovered slowly from the effects of Luke Clark's wet blanket, the following lyric, to the air of "The Minstrel Boy."—

THE BLUE CAP AND BUTTON.

The boys of the host that has suffered the most,
  The Army of the Potomac—
Who have dyed with their blood Virginia's fields
  To the color of the sumac;
There are some, you know, for McClellan will go—
  The "old braves," who still admire him;

While others for Meade will vote or bleed,
As the chances may require them.
CHORUS—The boys of the host, &c.

The lads in the West, whose luck is the best—
And gallantly still they carry it—
Are pledged to "Old Brains," who first gave them the reins
Of the victory winning chariot!
Twixt Halleck and Grant half doubting they pant;
And Rosy has friends, I augur,
Despite the mishap which put crape on his cap
By the banks of the Chickamauga.
CHORUS—The lads of the West, &c.

There is Dix and there's Banks who have friends in all ranks,
They are sons of the blue cap and button:
And with either, you see, any rival would be
Just as dead as a quarther of mutton!
But in West and in East there's one "black coat" at least,
Around whom the army might gather—
"Uncle Abe," it is you, honest, kindly and true—
To us boys you have been as a father!
CHORUS—There is Dix and there's Banks, &c.

HOW ARE THINGS IN NEW YORK?

Mr. Seward was anxious to know how things were going in New York. He had been gratified to see that in the November contest the Tammany and Mozart majority of over thirty thousand last year, had been so badly pulled down that one of their judicial candidates—Fernando Wood's brother-in-law—had been defeated; and that Judge McCunn, who was another, only claimed some fifty majority, while the impression was universal that his rival, Bosworth, had been defrauded out of a large legitimate majority by cheating in the Sixth ward.

Private O'Reilly answered that the Milesian settlement in question was "doin' as well as could be expected," as the gossips said when a lady was so ill that she could never be better until after she'd been worse. The few natives that were in the upper and western reserves of the island were kindly and humanely treated, "purvided only that they voted the reg'lar dimmycratic ticket and never axed for any places of official thrust." The same generous treatment had heretofore been extended to the Germans; but since they had set up a candidate of their own, in the person of Mr. C. Godfrey Gunther, they would hereafter be strictly confined, by order of the Common Council, to making bologna sausages, pretzel bunns, lager bier and rag picking. The managers of the Tammany-Mozart machines had brought things down to such a fine point that all nominations were now settled by a sociable game of "spoilt five" or "beggar-me-neighbor"—and faix! it was beggarin' the citizens, they was, at a two-forty rate, wid their tails over the dasher! "They tossed coppers for judgeships, dhrew sthraws for the State Legislature, and declared political death aginst anybody that wouldn't 'go straight' for their swindles. In ordher to give his misfortunate frind Luke Clark—as good a fellow at bottom, Misther Chase, as ever shuk toe at a wake or exercised his shillelagh and the privilege of a citizen at a primary election—he would now ask this honorable company to hear from Mr. Clark a song composed by Thomas Whelan, Esq., better known as 'Irish Tom,' who kept a whiskey coffee-house just opposite Collector Barney's Asylum for incurable imbeciles—it was, of course, the Custom House he meant." (Laughter and applause.)

MR. LUKE CLARK'S SECOND SONG.

Mr. Luke Clark thanked the company in general, and Misther Chase in particular, for the ginerosity and kindliness with which he was thrated. It would be well for Misther Sam Barlow to keep out of the way of his shillelagh when he got back to New York. It was down on the knees of his heart, he was axin' their pardon for his error; and now he'd like to tell them who Tom Whelan was before he gev them his song. Tom was a mimber of the Ancient and Honorable Society of St. Tammany. He had been a brave, with scalps at his girdle, whin the present Grand Sachems, Wiskinkies and Sagamores were no more than little papooses, swung in baskets over the backs of their mother-squaws. Tom had dhrunk as often from the Big Spring as ayther War Horse Purdy or Colonel Dan Delavan, that used to be City Inspecther. He had smoked the calumet in the best days of the party, and had hunted in their "Happy Huntin' Grounds." This song was a lament for the Tammany Society, addressed to Tom's great friend, Frank Boole, who is a good fellow at bottom, and a sound war dimmycrat, and who is supposed to be no more in love wid the "Raffle Managers" than Tom himself. Mr. Clark then cleared his throat and commenced roaring to the air of "The Widdy McGinness's Raffle:"—

THE LAMENT OF ST. TAMMANY.

Och, the times they are changed since as brothers we ranged,
Through our huntin' grounds happy and glorious;
When around the Big Spring every man was a king,
And the fun it was fast and uproarious;
Och, it's then we wor "braves," but it's now we are slaves,
Rough ridden at that wid a snaffle;
But our riders we'll taich, ere the goal they can raich,
We know tricks just worth two of their "raffle."
So sing this chorious, in pure Greek, gintlemin:
Sing Fal lal de ral al, &c.

God be wid the ould times, may they long live in rhymes,
Whin within the Ould Wigwam assembled,
Round the Council Fire set as full ayquils we met,
And before no Conthroller we thrembled!
O, them times will come back, or the thraces will crack,
And the coach be upset in the gravel;
For come good or come ill, curse the wan of us will
Submit any more to the "raffle!"
So sing, gintlemin, this chorious in choice Italian:
Fal de lal de ral al, &c.

O, we all lost a friend wid Bill Kennedy's end,
Thrue, honest, clear-headed, and hearty;
Little cared he for pelf; he was not for himself,
But was first and was last for the party!

O, soft on yer breast may the green verdure rest,
  Poor Bill! though aginst you they cavil—
These dogs, without soul, who now seek to conthrol
  Our party by mayns of their "raffle."
So sing, tindherly and slowly, boys dear, this German chorious:
  Fal de lal de ral, &c.

Take hands all around, let the melody sound,
  We are thrue to the flag and the nation;
Now let aich lift in air his good right hand, and swear
  Never more to submit to dictation!
To the divil we fling all the men of the "ring,"
  Who the party would bridle and snaffle;
And, if worst comes to worst, the "machines" will be burst—
  And 'tis we, boys, will hold the next raffle!
And, honeys, that sintimint is so thruly American, that we'll join in this native American chorious:
  Fal de lal ral de lal, &c.

Loud applause and laughter greeted this song, Mr. Chase sending his regards to Irish Tom and hoping that Father Murphy could give absolution to Mr. Clark for his many sins, as easily as he (Mr. Chase) gave him absolution for his greenback ditty.—(Laughter.)

Mr. Lincoln.—If Father Murphy could include Private O'Reilly in the same absolution, having special reference to the Lord Palmerston and Mrs.

O'Kane song, it should not be forgotten. (Loud Laughter.)

THE COUNT MERCIER'S SPEECH—A WAR CLOUD WITH GREAT BRITAIN.

The Count Mercier now pulled out his watch, and declared that the supreme, the ineffable, the inevitable moment had arrived! Standing here in the midst of the centuries—all the traditional splendors of the past pressing in upon his mental vision, and with all the possible glories of a French future for Mexico crowding with supernal presences and diaphoretic radiances in the foreground of his unutterable thoughts; thus standing, but not insensible to the material necessities on which French valor and French glory have their most enduring base, it became his duty to tell them that the supreme moment of dinner had arrived; and, as Madame the Comtesse had promised bully beef, fricaseed frogs and an oyster stew, he could by no means refuse to assist at the *celebration domestique.* Among the treasured memories of his future life should be the inconspicuous but not undelighted part which in this meeting he had borne. He would transmit to the *Memoire Diplomatique* his little joke about Lord Palmerston.

To his Imperial Majesty the Emperor, he would transmit Private O'Reilly's views about the succession; and it was his trust that the good fellowship of this interview would obviate any difficulties between the government which he had the honor to represent, and that of which, by many inches, Mr. Lincoln was the highest coronal. He would shake Private O'Reilly's hand! France thus embraced Hibernia! The Gauls and the Celts should be brothers; for they had a common faith, a common enemy. (Here he glanced towards Lord Lyons.) In this league of the Latin peoples, would not America join? It would be a point to rivet the eye of all history if Mr. Lincoln would condescend to take hands all round with Private O'Reilly and the speaker, as typical of the trinal unity and reconsolidated solidarity of the Latin race! If in this position they could dance the *cancan* together, singing as they circled round *mourir pour la patrie*, and *aux armes*, *aux armes*, *mes braves*, he thought the gigantic illustration of a mighty inter national thought would be complete. (Deep emotion, Lord Lyons very red, and making furious notes of the Count Mercier's words for transmission to his gov ernment.) Count Mercier saw what Lord Lyons was doing, and hurled against the implied threat of

English wrath that embalmed sublimity—that titanic but unspeakable word which, on the authority of Victor Hugo, in his book "Les Misérables," Colonel Cambronne, at the head of the last square of the old Imperial Guard at Waterloo, hurled against the English general who asked him to surrender.

MR. LINCOLN INTERFERES.

Mr. Lincoln begged the Count would not utter the word in question. As to dancing, he never danced. As to his being a candidate for re-election, that reminded him of what old Jesse Dubois once said to an itinerant preacher. Jesse, as State Auditor of Illinois, had charge of the State House at Springfield. The preacher asked the use of it for a lecture. "On what subject?" asked Jesse. "On the Millerite second coming of our Saviour," answered the long-faced man. "O, bosh," retorted Uncle Jesse, testily; "I guess if our Saviour had ever been to Springfield, and had got away with his life, he'd be too everlasting smart to think of coming here again." This was very much his case about the succession. As he saw they were buttoning up to go away, he would not seek to detain them—more especially as Louis Burgdorf had been making secret signs to him through the half open door, for the last half hour, that Mrs. Lincoln and the children would have cold turkey for their Thanksgiving dinner if he didn't cross over to the other side of the building. Good day, gentlemen [to the diplomatic corps and members of his Cabinet]. General Meagher, you, Private O'Reilly and Father Murphy will dine with me. O'Reilly's suggestion about the double stars shall not be forgotten."

CHAPTER X.

MILES O'REILLY IN RICHMOND.

REBEL VIEWS OF HIS RECEPTION BY PRESIDENT DAVIS.

From the Richmond Examiner (Pro-Beauregard anti-Davis organ), January 9th, 1863.

HISTORY will witness for us, though the personal adherents of the President seem unable to appreciate, how much we have borne and forborne during the last three years in deference to the high and difficult office of which, to the misfortune of the Confederacy, Mr. Jefferson Davis is the incumbent. No imagination can over-estimate the pecks of adverse opinion and the bushels of contempt we have swallowed in silence, rather than furnish any handle to the tools and pimps of the administration, for their oft-repeated and as often refuted slander, that our course is designed to embarrass the Government, and furnish aid and comfort to the enemy by a betrayal of domestic dissensions. It is high time, indeed, that this cry about "embarrassing the Government" should cease. It is, as Edmund Burke once said, "an attempt to convert the very confession of imbecility into a buckler against investigation, and thereby to secure a permanent continuance of the evil." Such pleas may avail the Yankee tyranny at Washington, but are wholly out of place amongst the people of this free and enlightened Confederacy. They may do for the organs, journalistic and Congressional, of the imperial and imperious despot who rules, reigns and riots over the destinies of the brutish and degraded North; but we tell Mr. Davis and his organs that the proud, brilliant, and chivalrous chieftains of the South despise and defy all such agencies for the suppression of their honest convictions.

In silence we have witnessed for over two years the efforts of our Government to break down and drive out of our service the General dearest to our people, and the most trusted champion of their cause. All know that General Beauregard has been under the ban of official jealousy ever since the first great victory of Bull Run. He was sent to command at Charleston as the readiest means of getting him out of the way—the calculation being, that if wooden vessels had forced, with so little loss, the more powerful defences guarding the approaches to New Orleans, how little could Beauregard do at Charleston against the vast flotilla of iron-clads which Mr. Davis knew, through our friends and emissaries in the North, to be then preparing for an attack upon the hated " cradle of Secession." Over all these calculations of his enemies, however, the genius of General Beauregard has triumphed; and this although the Tredegar foundries, under orders from our Secretary of War, refused to have cast for him the larger ordnance his requisitions certified to be necessary; and even went so far as to delay sending him the ordinary guns already cast until the full requisitions from every other commander in the field had been satisfied. Beauregard could not get a gun until the Davis pet, Pennsylvania Pemberton, had been supplied with all he needed, to hand over to the enemy at Vicksburgh. The Davis pet, Braxton Bragg, had also to be supplied with all the heavy artillery requisite to furnish abundant trophies to the Yankee Vandals in their entrance upon the various fortified positions which he successively abandoned. The defence of New Orleans was intrusted to another Davis pet—" a New York scavenger named Mansfield Lovell"—to quote the words of General

Pemberton — and with what result the country knows only too sadly!

But history, we say, will witness how patiently we have thus far kept silence on all the army blunders which have notoriously either caused our defeats, or rendered the most splendid achievements of our valor as fruitless as Lee's victory in the battle of the Wilderness, called by the Yankees "Chancellorsville;" or Bragg's partial successes—rather an opportunity for a victory than a victory itself—on the banks of the well-named Chickamauga.

We have seen the Confederacy cut in twain by the loss of the Mississippi river—the "Scavenger from New York" surrendering New Orleans without a blow; a Philadelphia incapable or traitor allowing himself, with one of our finest armies, to be cooped up within fortified lines at Vicksburgh, and starved into surrender by an army in the field, not much, if at all, superior to his own in numbers. We have seen Missouri and Arkansas lost by the fatal tendency of Mr. Davis to allow none but his own creatures to hold command. Sterling Price, the gallant and invincible, was superseded by General Heath, of Virginia; and Heath by Hindman; and Hindman by half a score of nameless others, who have since drunk themselves to death in bumpers to the health of Mr. Davis. The thrice chivalrous John Magruder has been exiled to Texas, with orders to "raise his own army if he wants one," because he threatened to break his sword when Yorktown was abandoned to McClellan without a blow; and because he could not see Bragg's policy of "falling back without a fight," whenever the enemy made any demonstration towards a flanking movement. A fellow called Finnegan, who talks Connemara Irish and doesn't know his horse's tail from his sabre, has been left in command of Florida for the last two years, and during that whole period has never organized one single attack upon the enemy, though with a force outnumbering theirs more than five to one. What true son of the Sunny South but blushes at our long record of unvaried disgrace and disaster in North Carolina? And now to sum up:—

Kentucky lost, Missouri lost, Arkansas lost, New Mexico and the Indian Territories lost, Mississippi lost, Tennessee lost, Alabama threatened and helpless; Georgia, with the foe in overwhelming force holding possession of her gates; Finnegan drinking whiskey slings with his staff and playing "old-sledge" on the top of an empty butter-firkin in the great Okeefinokee Swamp; North Carolina lying abject and unresisting before the Yankee raiders; Magruder without an army to meet Banks in Texas; Louisiana a prey to bogus conventions in which "colored Americans of African descent" are induced to vote for original signers of the Secession Ordinance; Georgia threatened in rear and neutralized on her coast-line by the enemy's possession of Fort Pulaski and the islands commanding the Wassaw and Ossibaw inlets; Western Virginia created a new State, and sending anti-slavery representatives to bow the supple hinges of the knee where thrift may follow fawning; while over all, upon a throne of Southern skulls—his long limbs swathed in robes of blood-dyed velvet, and holding the thigh-bone of Albert Sidney Johnson as a sceptre in his horrid hands—sits grimly the hideous Fetish who is the Yankee emperor!

And as if all this were not enough, to all these natural evils of war, evils of another kind are now being added, which seem to argue that the intellect of Mr. Davis is beginning to suffer under the neuralgic attacks which have of late grown so intense that he is often, his friends say, unable to sleep for as many as five days and nights in succession! We refer, of course, to the quasi-negotiations which he has allowed Mr. Ould, our commissioner, to hold with that Federal commander who has earned for himself the bad eminence of recognition by the title of "Beast Butler;" and to the still more flagrant folly and disgrace of his having granted a safe conduct from Savannah to Richmond, and from Richmond perhaps outside the Confederate lines, to a vulgar and insolent Irish Yahoo, who is ostensibly serving as a private soldier in the Yankee cohorts under General Gillmore, but to whom, nevertheless, President Davis has seen fit to accord the honors of an ambassadorial reception. We refer—and blush as we refer—to the reception granted by President Davis on last Sunday evening to private Miles O'Reilly, 47th Regiment New York Volunteers, now a part of the Yankee army of occupation on Morris and Folly Islands; and to the disgraceful scenes of riot and open treason, of which that visit was made the occasion, and of which a full report will be found elsewhere in our columns.

And who, we ask, after reading that report, can blame the "basin cats," the "Screamersville" vagabonds, the low Irish and Germans, and other *canaille* of Butchertown and Rockets, for their unseemly and scandalous proceedings? Who can wonder when it was noised abroad that this ridiculous and insulting envoy had arrived in town and was about to be received by President Davis, that all the "Union rats" should have come out of their holes and hailed with shouts and cheers, the hope of peace—even on the basis of "submission"—of which the reception of such an envoy appeared the certain augury? To Major Ben. Humphreys, the late Gen. John B. Floyd's worthy nephew, for his dignified rebuke to the self-abasement of Mr. Davis, we are indebted for the only redeeming feature in this disgraceful episode of our history. It is the old, old story:—"Le Roi s'amuse." Hector has lost his wits under wine and the Trojans suffer.

As to what passed between Mr. Davis and the envoy of the Washington tyrant, we, of course, are not in a position to give particulars if we would, nor would we if we could. The interview was held in the family residence of Mr. Davis, and not in the official chambers of the President of the Confederacy. Even for this slight favor we are thankful; for it will argue ill for the South whenever any individual in the uniform of the abhorred Union is allowed to stand, except as a manacled prisoner under sentence of death, in the Presidential presence upon Capitol Hill. As to the premature and indiscreet remarks indulged in by Colonel L. M. Keitt, Gov. John J. McRae, Lucius Q. C. Lamar, and Ex-Brigadier, now Private Pryor, in the bar-room of the Spottiswoode House—for which, as we learn, they were immediately confined in Castle Thunder—relative to the passage of an Act declaring Mr. Davis incompetent by reason of illness, thanking him for his services, allowing him a handsome pension to reside in Europe, and appointing Gen. Beauregard to fill the vacancy, *pro tem.*, we trust that nothing further will be done—at least at present. If, after full consideration, it be the judgment of our people that Mr. Davis has broken down under the burdens of his most onerous and harassing position, every thing that can be done should be done, to soften and make graceful his retirement; and until the people shall have declared otherwise by vote, Vice President Alexander Stephens must, to the grief of every true Confederate, be his successor! We speak of "the people" in this matter, not of Congress: for it is only too widely known that a majority of that body, either from weariness of the war, or devotion to the personal fortunes of Mr. Davis, are in favor of submitting proposals for Peace and re-Union to the Washington despotism whenever Mr. Jefferson Davis may either die or be removed.

In conclusion, before quitting this ridiculous and yet painful subject, let us hope that the advisers of Mr. Davis will have sense enough in themselves and weight enough with him, to prevent the return of this scandalous negotiator to the Federal lines. That he came under a flag of truce to Savannah, and was there received by Captain Gordon as a guest in the headquarters of General Mercer, is deplorably true: that, under a safe-conduct from President Davis, and in company with ex-General Gustavus W. Smith (whom we are surprised to find mixed up in such a business), he came from Savannah to this city, is also an unfortunate circumstance that cannot be denied. But in the inflammatory and diabolical speech which he made from the stoop of the Exchange Hotel to the "basin cats" and other vagabonds from Screamersville, Butchertown, and Rockets, who came to hear and cheer him; and still more in the diabolical songs with which he favored his congenial admirers upon that occasion, calling upon our gallant soldiery to mutiny, kill their officers, hang Congress, lay down their arms, and then pass quietly under the yoke—the Caudine forks ;—by these acts we claim, and the law of nations will support us in it (see Puffendorf, *Tome III. Cap.* 7, *Section* 25 ; Vattel, *Vol.* 5, *pages* 227–39 ; and Grotius, De Legibus Belli, *Vol. VI. Cap.* 22, *Section* 3), that he has forfeited the protection of his ambassadorial character and safe-conduct ; and we agree, at least thus far, with the gentlemen who have been imprisoned in Castle Thunder, that this last and worst insult of the tyrant Lincoln should be resented by the hanging of his congenial " envoy " on the highest gallows that can be erected on Capitol Hill ; and that, as was done in the cases of the three Scotch lords—Kilmarnock, Cromartie and Balmerino—in the Pretender's Rebellion of 1746, his entrails and heart be then taken out and burned ;—with the difference that, while theirs were wholly consumed in the fire and their ashes then scattered to the winds, the intestines and lights of this miscreant should only be cooked sufficiently to form a banquet for " Beast Butler," to whom, for his savory deglutition, they should then be transmitted under flag of truce.

ANOTHER VIEW OF MILES O REILLY'S RECEPTION.

(*From the Richmond Enquirer, official organ of Jeff. Davis.*)
JANUARY 10th, 1864.

Our friends of the *Examiner*, perhaps thinking it don't pay to keep cool this cold weather, have worked themselves up into the delirious condition of brain fever over an incident which has furnished to minds of better balance the most amusing and exhilarating topic of this carnival week. They see treason, stratagem and bloody spoils in the reception by President Davis of the latest edition of that magnificent farce—" Our Irish Ambassador."

To the proposition of the *Examiner* that the " intestines and lights" of Private Miles O'Reilly shall be cut out, roasted *à la maitre d'hotel*, and transmitted to General Butler "for his savory deglutition," we are perfectly willing to accede, whenever the proprietors of the paper in question, and that "gentleman from Ireland" who is their chief writer, will agree to present the dish in person to Gen. B. F. B., as did Herodias the head of John the Baptist to her mother!

It is an old saying, though we believe only true of the worst classes of our Milesian friends, that "you can never put one Irishman on a spit without finding half a dozen of his fellow-countrymen not only ready but eager to roast him;" and of this proverb, in its exceptional application, the *Examiner's* article upon this *ridiculus mus* affords a shining example. All its statements in the case are grossly erroneous, as we shall show hereafter—the naked facts that a person named Miles O'Reilly was received under flag of truce by Gen. Mercer at Savannah, accompanied to this city by ex-General Gustavus W. Smith, and that he has here been granted an interview with President Davis alone excepted.

And now let us ask the *Examiner* why did it not protest against the two audiences heretofore granted by President Davis to Dr. Zacharie, the celebrated corn-cutter and international negotiator, who has twice visited the South, ostensibly to see "his poor, dear old father, who lies (permanently) dying in Savannah;" but really as a semi-official agent of the Federal Government? Rumor says that Dr. Zacharie, during his first visit, was a guest on one occasion at the table of the *Examiner* people, adding that he was twice afterwards invited, but would not go, for the reason that a pickled pig's-head at the top of the table, pickled pig's feet at the foot, and four thin slices of broiled bacon as the *entremêts*, did not by any means form a pretty feast to set before a gentleman of his character.

Again, without going into a discussion of the obsolete theories laid down by Puffendorf, Grotius, and the other authorities recited by the *Examiner*, can we not admit—the United States being at least our equal—that President Davis can afford to receive any individual, no matter who or what, that President Lincoln can afford to send? Sir Walter Scott was no bad authority upon true chivalry, and in the mouth of Lord Marmion he has put a quotation completely decisive of this point:—

"And first I tell thee, haughty peer!
He who does England's message here,
Were he the meanest in her state,
May well, proud Angus! be thy mate."

As for ourselves, between Dr. Zacharie and Private O'Reilly, we are clearly in favor of the latter. If we were in the Washington government's place, perhaps neither might be sent; but *chacun à son gout*—as the old woman said when she kissed her cow.

In the *Examiner's* charges that Private O'Reilly made a speech of the most inflammatory character to the "basin-cats" and other *canaille* from Butchertown and Screamersville, "who had assembled to hear and cheer him;" and that he sang to the same crowd from the stoop of the Exchange Hotel, songs advising our gallant soldiers to mutiny, kill their officers and then submit quietly to the jugurthan yoke—there is, need we say, not one syllable of truth? His speech was purely humorous in character, and—as we have heard from some who were present—in very excellent taste for the occasion, all subjects of difference being avoided as much as possible. He spoke with true Irish pathos of former happy days in the South, through which, it appears, he roamed pretty extensively, some ten years ago, as "deputy aide-de-camp" to a Yankee pedlar of cheap jewelry, gold pens and other "notions."

The song about Northern and Southern soldiers was given on the invitation of Messrs. Boteler, Brokenborough, De Jarnette and other gentlemen of equally high character, who had collected on the Exchange stoop to hear and be amused; and if he did wrong in singing it, he erred on the invitation of gentlemen whose loyalty to the Confederate flag is, to say the very least, as unimpeachable as that of the *Examiner*. The main part of his audience, we may here say, were neither "basin-cats," nor *ca-*

naille, but out-door hospital-patients and veterans from Lee's army home on furlough. Will our citizens believe that to such an audience any song of the kind described by the *Examiner* could be sung with impunity?

So far was this lyric from containing anything improper for Southrons to hear from a Northern soldier, that we gladly print it, as a refutation of the *Examiner's* slander, from a copy in the hands of Gen. Winder, who has charge of Private O'Reilly at the Exchange Hotel. To our way of thinking, it shows a kindlier feeling on the part of our Northern foemen to the soldiers of the South, than we were prepared to expect; and if such be—as Private O'Reilly claims—a fair example of the sentiments of the great mass of the Federal "blue-bellies," it evinces, we think, a disposition towards a restoration of Peace and Brotherhood, on terms not only honorable and just to both sides, but also presenting a dream of "Universal Dominion," which we know to have long lain close to the hearts of the whole American people before the commencement of this unhappy civil war.

Of this lyric Private Miles denies the authorship, saying that it was written by "a great scholar all out," named Corporal Tracy, who is now, or was when Miles last heard from him, senior orderly at Gen. John A. Logan's head-quarters. Tracy, it appears, was badly wounded at Gettysburgh, and had to lie for some weeks in a field-hospital, wherein Confederate and Union soldiers were mixed up indiscriminately. It was there and thus that Tracy wrote; and as his verses were sung by Private O'Reilly to the air of "Jamie's on the Stormy Sea," there were many kindling eyes and heaving hearts amongst the veterans in his audience. It was entirely pathetic, and yet entirely manly. The *vieux moustaches*, familiar with the sounds of battle, caught the echoes of old fights in all its swelling lines and sinking cadences; and the suggestion in the last stanza that North and South should reunite to wipe out our "common wrongs" with France and England, was rapturously applauded.

He called it:

THE BLUE-BELLIES TO THE GREY-BACKS.

A DREAM OF UNIVERSAL DOMINION.

Men who have, in many a battle,
Made the hail round either rattle,
Keeling over men and cattle,
  Souls and bullets on the wing;—

Must this war, its woes expanding,
Still be pushed, fresh lives demanding,
We like gladiators standing
  Elbow-bloodied in the ring?

Grape-shot rustling, bullets singing,
Round shot humming, orders ringing,
And our torn, loved flags a-swinging,
  Forward in the fiery gales;—
Bugles fiercely, sharply sounding,
Sheets of flame the sight confounding,
And, o'er all, the heavy pounding
  Of the red artillery flails!

Brethren, thus we stand confronted,
Every bayonet forward slanted,
Tired and bloody but undaunted—
  Shall the work again begin?
Shall the cry again be slaughter,
Your blood, our blood shed like water—
Pitiless and useless slaughter,
  In a fight ye cannot win?

Curse the symbols that divide us,
Folly and fraud alone divide us,
Brethren, join us—stand beside us—
  Both have wrongs to wipe away;
All our feuds forgotten, ended,
Let our flag, with forces blended,
O'er the world, serene and splendid,
  Henceforth bear imperial sway!

As to the "premature and indiscreet remarks" made by Messrs. Keitt, Lamar, Curry, McRae, and Private Roger A. Pryor in the bar-room of the Spottiswoode House, relative to deposing President Jeff. Davis and elevating General Beauregard to his place, we have little to say at present—except to express our sincere joy that this scheme, so long festering in the minds of that little clique represented by the *Examiner*, has thus been brought to a head that can be seen and punctured. For Col. Keitt we are sorry. As commander of Fort Wagner, he fought bravely and held out with conspicuous resolve. McRae and Curry have of late so broken down their constitutions, that whiskey takes effect on them after the second quart—a thing it never did before. Lamar is a hot-headed and shallow dreamer, whose appointment as Professor of Philosophy by the Mississippi University, was one of the most magnificent satires ever devised against the miserable muddle and trash of ethical and metaphysical acquirements. As to Pryor, formerly a Brigadier, but reduced for sufficient cause to the ranks, he is a born and bred conspirator—a natural Marat, to whom no mercy should be shown; and in his case we respectfully urge that President Davis owes it to the country to apply the advice given gratis by the *Examiner* in regard to the hanging of Private O'Reilly, and the burning by the common hangman of his lights and bowels. When executions of this just character begin, we caution all the rest of the Anti-Davis people not to be found too near the gallows!

Of the only other song given by Private Miles O'Reilly, from the stoop of the Exchange Hotel, we have just received a copy from Mayor Mayo, who was also one of the "basin-cat" audience described by the *Examiner*. This song is said to be the work of a Yankee officer attached to the Ordnance Corps, named Horace Porter, whose Teutonic version of "King Dickey de trèe times"—Shakespeare's Richard the Third,—as given in a Dutch district of Pennsylvania—will long be remembered by all our young West Pointers who were Cadets at the same time with Captain Porter. Private Miles sang the words with great spirit and tenderness to the air of "Napoleon's March," the soldiers in his audience appearing much pleased with it, and giving it an enthusiastic *encore*. He called it:

THE REVIEW.

A PICTURE OF OUR VETERANS.

"Morituri te salutant,"
Say the soldiers as they pass;
Not in uttered words they say it,
But we feel it as they pass;
"We, that are about to perish,
We salute you as we pass!"

Gallant chiefs their swords presenting,
Trail them proudly as they pass;
Battle banners, torn and glorious,
Dip, saluting, as they pass:
Brazen clangors shake the welkin
As the marching columns pass.

Naught of golden pomp, or glitter,
Marks the veterans as they pass;
Travel-stained, but bronzed and sinewy,
Firmly, proudly on they pass;
And we hear them—"Morituri
Te salutant," as they pass.

On his pawing steed the General
Scans the waves of men that pass;
And his eyes at times are misty,
Then are blazing as they pass;

And his breast with pride is heaving
As the stalwart veterans pass.

* * * * * * * * a *

Oh, our comrades! gone before us
  In the last review to pass,
Never more to earthly chieftain
  Dipping colors as you pass;—
Heaven accord you gentle judgment
  When before its Throne you pass!

To the souls of all our perished
  We, who still saluting, pass,
Dip the flag and trail the sabre
  As with wasted ranks we pass;—
And we murmur, "Morituri
  Vos salutant," as we pass!

To whatever of "high treason against the Confederacy" the *Examiner* can find in this last quaint and uncouth, but touching and soldierly song, we bid it welcome. Already it is on the lips and in the hearts of many of our veterans; and we believe they will fight none the worse for it when Lee's or Johnson's bugles again arouse them to strike tents, pack ten days' rations, and march northward or westward to repel the foul Yankee invader.

In the mission of Private O'Reilly we see the rays, and the only rays yet vouchsafed to our straining sight, of a peaceful dawn. When the Yankee

Government sends us an Envoy of this kind, it is proof that it must be thinking of making, of its own motion, some concessions of one sort or the other, while officially demanding of us absolute submission. In a word, Mr. Lincoln appears ready, if we can judge from the tone of his only accredited minister, Private Miles O'Reilly, to "build a bridge of gold" for our leaders to retreat over. He will at least give them a canoe to go ashore on, before asking them to scuttle their own ship and let her sink, without further effort, into the darkness and oblivion which are the meed of all unsuccessful great national struggles.

CHAPTER XI.

MILES O'REILLY AT FORTRESS MONROE.

(Suppressed Dispatch to the N. Y. Herald.)

FORTRESS MONROE, January 13, 1864.

BY the flag of truce boat "New York," from City Point, this morning arrived Private Miles O'Reilly, 47th Regiment New York Volunteers, *en route* from Richmond to Washington with important dispatches. Private O'Reilly appears in good health and remarkably good appetite—the latter probably a result of his brief sojourn within the Confederate lines. He says himself that he "was treated as well as they knew how, and could afford, poor craythurs;" and that his heart bled for many of them whom he had known in better and more peaceful times. Of their condition, or what he thinks of the treatment of our prisoners, he will give no picture, indignantly spurning all questions, on the ground that his appointment as the successor of Dr. Zacharie has placed him in a confidential position between

Mr. Jefferson Davis and His Excellency the President of the United States; and that what he has seen and heard "is the business of them two, and of no one else whatsumdever."

Immediately on the arrival of Private O'Reilly he was surrounded by a vast crowd of soldiers, citizens and sailors, who cheered him vociferously, calling—some for a speech, others for a song; but to none of these requests would he accede. Shaking hands with all, but elbowing his way vigorously through them, and towards the sally-port of the Fortress, he was at length released by the interposition of Colonel J. Wilson Shaffer, Chief of Staff to General Butler, who took him in charge, and ordered the assemblage to fall back—a mandate enforced by a sergeant and squad of men sent down to compel order.

Private O'Reilly was introduced to General Butler by Colonel Shaffer, who said that he had known Miles for years, having formerly had him under his command in Missouri, Kansas and the Indian Territories—under Frémont in the former Department; and, in the latter, about the time that Colonel (now General) Canby made his gallant fight, and suffered so severely, at the battle of Fort Craig.

General Butler said he was glad to see Private

Miles, and immediately ordered Colonel Shaffer to prepare a special dispatch steamer to carry the new "Envoy Extraordinary"—General Butler said "extraordinary envoy"—to Baltimore, where a special train for Washington would be in waiting. "No one can tell, Shaffer," said General Butler, "what's going to be the upshot of this Miles O'Reilly business! He is worth a dozen Zacharies; and the rebels may have 'acknowledged the corn' to him which they concealed from the corn-cutter." With these words General Butler withdrew O'Reilly into his private office, from which they did not again emerge until Colonel Shaffer tapped at the door and reported the dispatch-boat nearly ready.

By this time the whole garrison had assembled in front of the General's headquarters; and the appearance on the stoop of Private Miles in company with General Butler, was the signal for a burst of cheering that made the welkin ring. "Order him to speak, General—order him to sing," were the prevailing cries, mingled with cheers for "Butler," "Honest Old Abe," "General Grant," "Little Mac," "Sal. Chase," "Admiral Du Pont," and other eminent characters who live in the hearts of the soldiery and people.

General Butler, introducing Miles, desired them to know that he had seen Private O'Reilly before. It was at the Charleston Convention, where Miles had been "going his millions better with nary a pair" on the lamented Stephen A. Douglas; while he (Gen. Butler), in company with the late Isaac I. Stevens, then delegate from Oregon, was working like a beaver for Breckinridge (groans), or whomsoever else the "black squadron of the Gulf States" would agree upon as their candidate. (Dead silence.) His friend Gen. Stevens had since been paid with a bullet through his brain for that attempted service to the cause of the South. He was shot while carrying the colors of the 79th New York Highlanders—his old regiment—in an attempt to retrieve Gen. Pope's disasters in front of Washington. (Loud cheers.) As for himself (Gen. Butler), he had seen the error of his ways and claimed that he had brought forth fruits meet for repentance. (Loud laughter and cheers.) It was now his chief regret that his old friend and co-operator, Caleb Cushing, still remained in a condition of Egyptian darkness—at least, had returned to that condition ever since Mr. Lincoln had refused his repeated applications for a Brigadier's commission; and ever since he had realized how much money could be made by prosecuting claims against Uncle Sam in the interest of the shoddy contractors and copperheads. (Laughter and cheers renewed.)

General Butler would only further remark, before introducing to his audience Private O'Reilly, that he had often been struck by recognising amongst the names of the anti-Douglas leaders in the Charleston Convention, nearly all those arch-villains upon whom the hand of Heaven and an outraged country now presses with heaviest terrors. (Loud cheers.) Some of them lie in bloody and nameless graves—and these are the happiest. Some are exiles in Europe, penniless, despised, and without hope—Uncle Sam's soldiers in possession of their palaces and plantations; themselves the laughing-stock of diplomacy. Some have drunk, and others are drinking themselves to death—seeking in oblivion, at any cost, an escape from the haunting spectres of the human hecatombs that have been sacrificed to their ambition. (Sensation and applause.) Upon the brows of all, the brands of the wrath of God and man are visibly imprinted. Famished, ragged, hollow-eyed, foot-sore, and fainting, the few survivors of the original conspiracy at Charleston now drag themselves round their desolated country at the head of diminishing legions—cursed everywhere in the hearts of their less guilty, because more ignorant dupes; and terrified by the vision in a near future of that Divine Retribution which gave up to the guillotine in Paris, and by the very hands of the Jacobin-mob who had been their frenzied idolators and instruments—the authors of the worst infamies of the Reign of Terror. (Sensation and cheering.) General Butler would now introduce Private Miles O'Reilly, 47th Regiment New York Volunteers, who could only address them very briefly, the steamer being nearly if not quite ready; and O'Reilly's business with the President (loud cheers) being of a kind that could not be delayed. (Cheers, and a voice: "Nine times nine for our next President.")

Private Miles, on stepping forward, thanked General Butler and Col. Shaffer for their kindness, which he regarded as wholly undeserved by any thing he had done or could do. [Loud cries of "You're too modest, Miles," and laughter.] Of how he had come to be within the Rebel lines, and how he had got out of them, the bundle of Southern papers he had brought would give them particulars, if they would only read "Extracts from the Southern press," in the next day's *Herald*. But on his way that morning in the flag-of-truce boat from City Point, he had picked up an old New York paper containing a debate in the Senate of the United States that "made a fool of all the other debates" he had ever seen. "To the rare—open ordher—march," shouted he in stentorian accents. "Prepare for review! It isn't a review of yourselves, boys, I mane, so don't be pullin' your white cottons out of your pockets; but it's a review of that illusthrious Conschrip Father, who is opposed to axin' any questions of Uncle Gid., as to how he spinds the nate little sum of nearly two hundhred millions a year, for a navy that can't catch the 'Alabama;' while at the same time, this same Conschrip Father—an' I wish he *was* conschripted wid all my heart—is in favor of again cuttin' down the pay of our officers,—and this although they are now paid in a currency that isn't as good by a long sight as its face!" In honor of this conscript Father, he would give them a song, written by Captain De Lancy Rochford, of the Invalid Corps, formerly of the Irish Brigade,—only premising for the benefit of such misfortunates as hadn't had the privilege of being born in Ireland, that the words of the chorus, "*Ma bouchal dhas cruithin amoe*," meant "My pretty boy milking his cow," as "Ma colleen dhas," in the original, meant the other gender. He begged all present to join him in the chorus, which should be accompanied by the gesture of "milking," and which must be pronounced as if spelled: "*Ma boohal tha crooveen amoe.*" [Uproarious laughter and cries of "We will that, Miles."] "Just to think of it," continued Private O'Reilly, waxing indignant, "just to think that while the financial stump-tail only yields us a swill-milk currency, not only is the army to suffer from the natural wakeness of the demoralized liquid, but even the small quantity honestly due us is to be cut down!' [Loud cries of "Grimes shan't do it, Miles," &c.]

"So now, boys," resumed Miles, "get your right hands ready for milkin', and when I give the signal for the chorious, rattle down the fluid lively into your tin pails. I tell yez all, that no candydate need hereafther apply for the Irish vote, or the army or navy vote, who can't sing this song and give the pure Greek chorious its thrue Athaynian accintuation."

A HEALTH TO THE MAN FROM I-OW-A.

AIR:—*The Pretty Boy Milking his Cow.*

Here's a health to the man from I-ow-a,
  The popular saver o' dimes!

On the thrumpet o' fame let us blow a
  Loud pæan in honor o' Grimes!
Wid his hand on the navy's full uddher,
  He can make the crame goldenly flow,
Of Gid's ark he's the pilot an' ruddher,
  Ma bouchal dhas cruithin amoe!

Chorus (*all milking as if for dear life*),

Wid his hand on the Navy's full uddher
  He can make the crame goldenly flow,
Of Gid's ark he's the pilot an' ruddher,
  Ma bouchal dhas cruithin amoe!

His frindship for Gid is amazin',
  The navy's defects must be hid,
For he shwears 'tis misprishin o' thrayson
  To ax any questions o' Gid:—
But he'll pinch from the Captains an' Kurnils,
  Some quarthers an' dimes, as we know,
An' be puffed by "intilligent journals,"
  Ma bouchal dhas cruithin amoe!

Chorus (*milking hard and rattling the fluid down into their tin pails as directed*),

But he'll pinch, from the Captains an' Kurnils,
  Some quarthers an' dimes, as we know,
An' be puffed by "intilligent journals,"
  Ma bouchal dhas cruithin amoe!

Poor divils who wear sash an' sabre,
  Prepare to be docked o' your dimes—

What is all your hard fightin' and labor,
Compared wid the value o' Grimes?
Republics we know are desayteful—
The story was told long ago—
But Gid is both mighty an' grateful,
Ma bouchal dhas cruithin amoe!

Chorus (*milking as if resolved to pull the teats off the imaginary stump tail*),
Republics we know are desayteful—
The story was told long ago—
But Gid is both mighty an' grateful,
Ma bouchal dhas cruithin amoe.

Never was song a greater success than this, despite the very execrable and Fort Lafayetty "tang" that was in some of what Ben. Shillaber, as "Mrs. Partington" would call—"its seditionary sediments." The audience "milked" and roared until the very sentinels caught the infection and shook all over as they presented arms to passing double-rows of buttons. Gen. Butler had a cough so violent that it compelled him to cover his face with his handkerchief. Col. Shaffer took refuge behind a pillar, and internally determined that Miles should some day or other be his guest "at Freeport, Illinoy"—of which rising, but not yet quite risen town, he was mayor, sheriff, county clerk, register, and both boards of the common council at last advices. It is even said that an orderly sergeant of the regular army—that stateliest and most solemn of created beings—was observed to bite very hard on a bullet which he carries round in his pocket to guard against the rare temptation of a smile : but even the bullet couldn't save him. He first smiled, then grinned ; and finally the infection of the universal "milking" so carried him away, that he was actually seen to pull the imaginary teat of the Treasury stump-tail no less than thrice during the third chorus !

Emerging at last from behind the pillar, Col. Shaffer was understood to observe—running his fingers wildly through his hair as he spoke—that the song was improper, and should not have been sung. It was a thing to be deplored. [Here the Colonel choked, coughed, and blew his nose.] He had no time, however, to call their attention at present to that portion of the "Revised Army Regulations" applying to the case. The steamboat was waiting ; the President was waiting ; the Country was waiting ; and Private Miles had no time to lose. On behalf of General Butler, who had retired, he thanked the crowd for their conduct—with the exception of their having laughed at a chorus (here the Colonel "milked") which should rather have moved their tears. [Loud laughter, the crowd recommencing to "milk" and again shouting "Ma bouchal dhas cruithin amoe!"] All present would now retire, while he and Private O'Reilly made their way to the boat.

Upon this Colonel R. M. Hough, of Chicago, stepped forward and shook Private O'Reilly by the hand. "Miles," said he—with many expletives omitted—"Miles, I love you. You've a heart bigger, Miles, than any steer I ever slaughtered. I've killed and packed more steers in my time, and I've had more bullets fired at me at one moment, than any other man this side of—no matter where! But amongst all the steers, Miles, and I've weighed their hearts, there never was a bigger heart than yours!" [Applause from the crowd, Colonel Hough being now at the Fortress filling a beef contract.] "Before he goes, Shaffer, I've one favor to ask: that you'll give him time for a song that I hear he once wrote about some celebrated steers in South Carolina. If you'll only do this, old fellow, I'll stand two baskets!"

Colonel Shaffer consented—the more readily, as the dispatch-boat had not yet completed her coaling. "Now fire away, Miles," urged the impatient Hough. "I've had once to run Shaffer and a saw-mill, Gen.

Benham and a coal-yard, all four together; I've had a horse fall under me with sixteen bullets in his body, twenty-two bullets through my clothes, and only a scratch on my sitting-machine. I've charged on horseback into the sea to fight an iron-clad ; but"—and here the Colonel became very energetic in his assurances—" a song from you about a live steer, or a dead steer for the matter of that, would more than repay me for all I have been, and done, and suffered in the suppression of this most foul and unnatural rebellion."

Private O'Reilly, whose face brightened up at the hint about " two baskets," briefly explained that the South Carolina " steer" happened to be a " bull ;" and the only bull, on the authority of a celebrated elderly and philanthropic lady, to be found in all the Sea-Islands of the Southern coast at the time of his lamented decease. Certain straggling soldiers had crossed over from St. Helena to Lady's Island one day, and in sport had made beef of the bull. [Laughter.] Not such " prime mess," to be sure, as Col. Hough was in the habit of slaughtering, but ordinary army beef—or beef without much bleeding, by the process of bullets. It was to lay before General Hunter this disaster to the cows under her charge, that the eminent philanthropic lady, already referred to, next morning wrote and sent to Head Quarters of the Department the subjoined elegy, which (as alleged) she offered to appear and sing, if so desired, to the air that "The Old Cow died of." It was called:

THE BUTCHERED BULL.

A BALLAD OF LADY'S ISLAND.

Dear General H., my heart is full
  Lamenting for my butchered bull;
The only bull our islands had,
  And all my widowed cows are sad.

With briny tears and drooping tails,
  And loud boo-hoos and bovine wails,
My kine lament with wifely zeal
  Their perished hopes of future veal.

Sad is the wail of human wife
  To see her partner snatched from life;
But he, the husband of a score,
  For him the grief is more and more!

Henceforth no hope of golden cream—
  Even milk in tea becomes a dream;
Whey, bonnyclabber, cheese and curds,
  Are now, ah, me! mere idle words.

The cruel soldiers, fierce and full
  Of reckless wrath, have shot my bull;
The stateliest bull—let scoffers laugh—
  That e'er was "Father" called by calf.

A bull as noble, firm and fair
  As that which aided Jove to bear
Europa from the flowery glade
  Where she, amidst her maidens, played.

So, General dear, accept my vows,
  And oh! take pity on my cows,
With whom, bereft of wifely ties,
  All tender hearts must sympathize.

Quick to the North your order send
  (By Smith's congenial spirit penned),
And order them, in language full,
  At once to send me down a bull:—

If possible, a youthful beast,
  With warm affections yet unplaced,
Who to my widowed cows may prove
  A husband of undying love.

The recitation of this elegy concluded, Private O'Reilly, preceded by Colonels Shaffer and Hough, made his way to the steamboat pier, and was soon *en route* for Washington, charged with information for the President, and carrying with him renewed pleasant recollections of "life at old Point Comfort." To the President and Congress we now commit him and the important "Proposals for Peace," about which Mr. Fernando Wood is continually raving in Congress, and of which, we assure him, Miles O'Reilly is the only authorized bearer.

What these "Peace" proposals are, it is for Mr. Lincoln to explain, whenever such explanation can be given "consistently with the public interests." In Mr. Lincoln's hands we are well assured, that, whenever the negotiation ripens to a consistency that will give us back "Peace with the Union," all minor points of difference or difficulty will be ignored. The cocoa-nut will be laid, in its layers of native packing, upon the Speaker's desk. Messrs. Anson Herrick, of New York, better known as "the Deacon;" and S. S. Cox, of Ohio, better known as "Sun-Set," will be appointed a Committee of two to piece one of the eyes of the fruit, and let not only Fernando, but all the country, taste its milk! Private O'Reilly will then appear as "ma bouchal dhas cruithin" his cocoanut—there being no word in Holy Irish for this heathen fruit; and, with both houses of Congress singing, sipping, and "milking," Brother Ben will lie down with Owen Lovejoy; Mr.

Holman, of Indiana, take Thad. Stevens of Pennsylvania as the partner of his couch; while Sunset Cox will get astride of war-horse Gurley, and allow that mild but mettled animal to snuff "Peace anear" with the same keen nostrils that were once distended in the task of snuffing battles—at a distance! The golden age will return, and Mr. Chase will re-employ Jay Cooke & Co. in buying up greenbacks all over the country, giving twenty-three dollars and fifty cents in gold for every ten dollars' worth of the verdant paper that has on it the quaint signature of General Spinner. For this agency the patriotic financiers named will charge nothing; after which, it will only remain to proclaim that the Millennium which was to have arroven, has arriv; and that Private Miles O'Reilly, 47th Regiment New York Volunteers, has been its *præsidium et dulce decus*—at once its poet and its prophet!

THE END.

Mrs. Mary J. Holmes' Works.

MARIAN GREY.—A Novel. . . . 12mo. cloth bound, $1.25
'LENA RIVERS.— . . . . do. $1.25
MEADOW BROOK.— . . . . . . do. $1.25
HOMESTEAD ON THE HILLSIDE.— . do. $1.25
DORA DEANE.— . . . . do. $1.25
COUSIN MAUDE.— . . . . do. $1.25
DARKNESS AND DAYLIGHT.—(In press.) do. $1.25

Artemus Ward.

HIS BOOK.—An irresistibly funny volume of writings by the immortal American humorist and showman; with plenty of comic illustrations to match. . 12mo. cl. bound, $1.25

Miss Augusta J. Evans.

BEULAH.—A novel of great power and interest. Cl. bd., $1.50

Richard B. Kimball.

WAS HE SUCCESSFUL?— A novel. 12mo. cl. bound, $1.50
UNDERCURRENTS.— . . . do. do. $1.50
SAINT LEGER.— . . . . do. do. $1.50
ROMANCE OF STUDENT LIFE.— do. do. $1.25
IN THE TROPICS.—Edited by R. B. Kimball. do. $1.25

Cuthbert Bede.

THE ADVENTURES OF VERDANT GREEN.—A rollicking, humorous novel of student life in an English University; with more than 200 comic illustrations. . 12mo. cl. bd., $1.25

Edmund Kirke.

AMONG THE PINES.—A thrilling picture of life at the South. 12mo., paper covers, 75 cts., . . or cloth bound, $1.00
MY SOUTHERN FRIENDS; OR, LIFE IN DIXIE.—12mo., paper covers, 75 cts., ... or cloth bound, $1.00
WHAT I SAW IN TENNESSEE.—Paper, 75 cts., or cl. bd., $1.00

The Central Park.

THE ORIGIN, PROGRESS, AND DESCRIPTION, OF THE MAGNIFICENT CENTRAL PARK AT NEW YORK.—Beautifully illustrated with more than 50 exquisite photographs of the principal views and objects of interest. One large quarto, sumptuously bound in . . . . Turkey morocco, $25.00

Ernest Renan.

THE LIFE OF JESUS.—Translated from the original French by C. E. Wilbour. . . . . 12mo. cloth bound, $1.50

www.ingramcontent.com/pod-product-compliance
Lightning Source LLC
LaVergne TN
LVHW020056110826
845151LV00005B/1493

* 9 7 8 1 4 2 5 5 2 1 9 6 7 *